AF344941

LIVING IN PARADISE

97 TIPS FOR ARCHITECTS

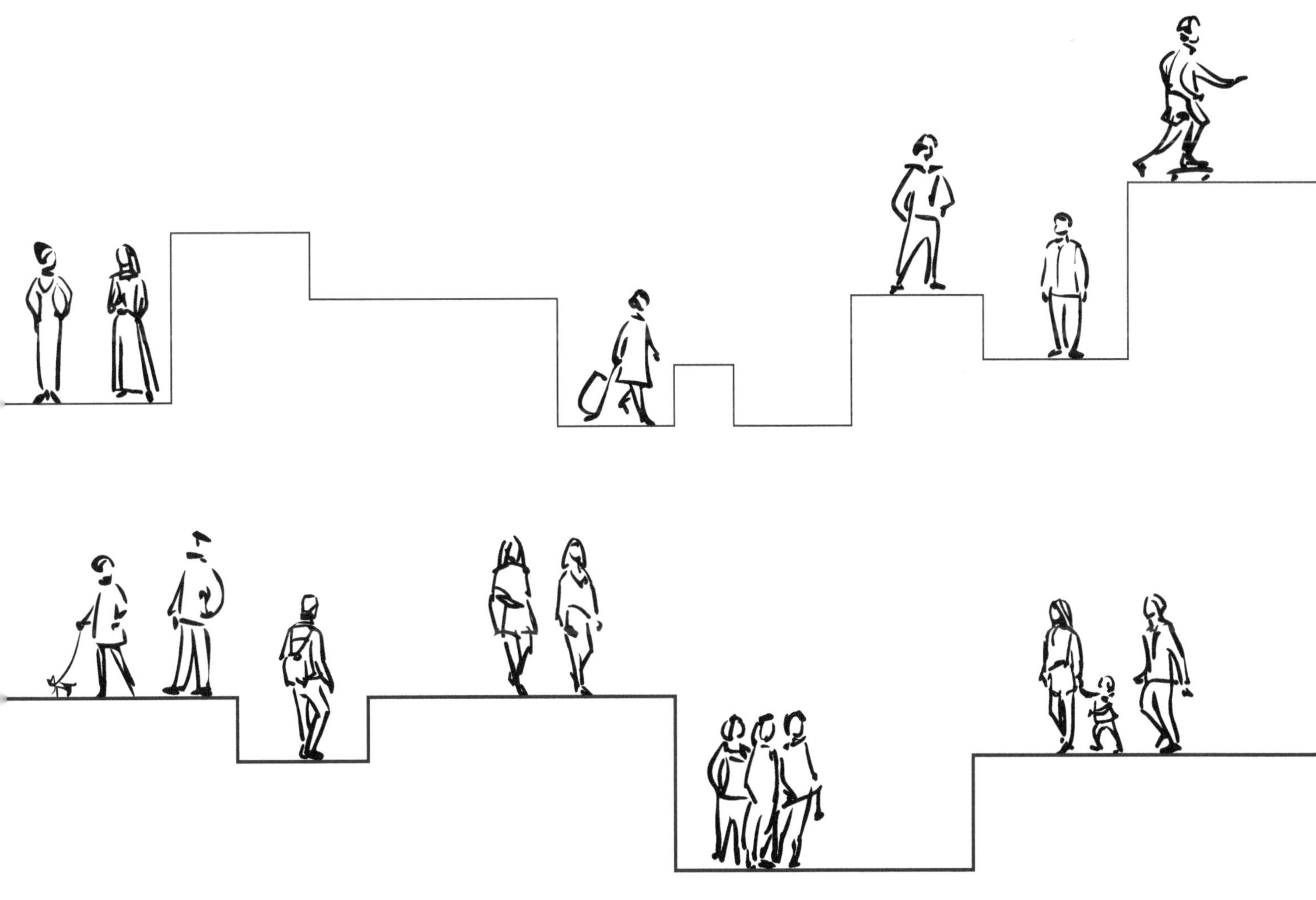

Ondrej Slunecko

BUREAU | BOUJEE

Dear reader, thank you very much for opening this book. I hope
it will bring you lots of joy and valuable information.

Enjoy!

ISBN: 978-80-270-7652-9
Keywords: Architecture, architect, design, urbanism, city, human scale, home, interior, construction

Author's Note

Architecture is the most beautiful endeavour I have ever encountered. There is something magical about being able to shape the world around you. It is a nourishment for your ego and exercise for your mind. It gives you hope that the world can be a better place when you cease to exist and it gives you a chance to leave something of a value behind.

I would call it a quest for beauty. We must look for the beauty in the world and reflect it in architecture, in order for other people to see the world as we see it.

However, all this comes at a price. If you want an easy life, don't be an architect. The adjectives that can describe architecture are these; ruthless, complicated, unforgiving, difficult, limiting and messy. First and foremost your freedom is severely limited by clients, laws and functional requirements. There might be many years between the moment of the first idea and the handing over of the building. The process is painfully long and in the end, how many buildings do you think you can build in your lifetime? Twenty? People will try to stop you, or worse, they will want you to make a compromise. Hence, you need to persuade those people. And that is going to drain a lot of energy from you.

However, in the end, when you see, that you were able to imprint your hopes and dreams into concrete, wood, glass and steel by influencing less than one-fifth of parameters, only then will you realize that it was all worth it.

About the book

Architecture is awfully chaotic. There are thousands of sources of information and hundreds of approaches on how to design. This book is neither a guide nor a comprehensive source of data. It is the essence of architecture as I see it. Messy, disorganized collection. Shards of wisdom I collected over the years. From books, colleagues, teachers, lectures and famous architects. Some of them I even discovered myself.

I found out that often, it takes a whole lecture to introduce one concept. Or that a book has two hundred pages to explain four core ideas. Famous architects also often repeat one trick over and over. Therefore, I took the notes I collected over the course of my career and summed up the most interesting ideas into short and clear tips.

They are laid there, one after the other. Each tip accompanied by an illustration which is at least tangentially connected to the tip itself. Illustrations have many different styles since I am unable to stick with one and I get bored easily. To further emphasize this, I invited some of my dear friends to help me and illustrate some of the tips.

Actually some tips might even be contradictory to other tips. That is how it works in architecture. There is more than one right way of doing things. Actually, I love when people disagree with me, so I encourage you to write me your opinions about the book and each particular tip if you want to. The tips are plenty and if you will like this book, there might be at least one more to come.

The opposites attract

As architects, we even have a fancy word to use; juxtaposition. When you place two components close to each other and there is a difference between them, (texture, size, orientation, colour) they emphasize each other. How could you appreciate smoothness of velvet without ever bruising your knee on a sidewalk?

Setting opposites side by side creates tension. And as we observed from human interaction, tension is a good thing.

Observe materials and their properties to enhance their composition.

Never fell a tree

Being an architect is not just a job, it is an opportunity to make the right decision for others to follow. Sure, there might be times when it will be necessary to interrupt nature, in those cases make sure that the trees will be replanted elsewhere.

Consider weaving your design among the trees or planting new if your project is on a barren land. The seeds we sow today will bring us joy in the years to come.

Respect the street wall

Buildings create a positive space along the street edge and shape the spatial continuity. Even though it might be tempting to place the front facade of an infill building with a setback from the existing street wall, consider the negative effects it may bring. It reduces the profitability, accessibility and weakens the spatial integrity of the whole street.

Never stop playing

The fascinating thing about children is, that they will never tell you something cannot be done. Nobody ever told them. Thus, they try what seems to be impossible to others.

You should approach problems with the same naivety. Look at problem you are facing without assumptions, study it carefully and test possibilities that might lead nowhere. You will be surprised by the result.

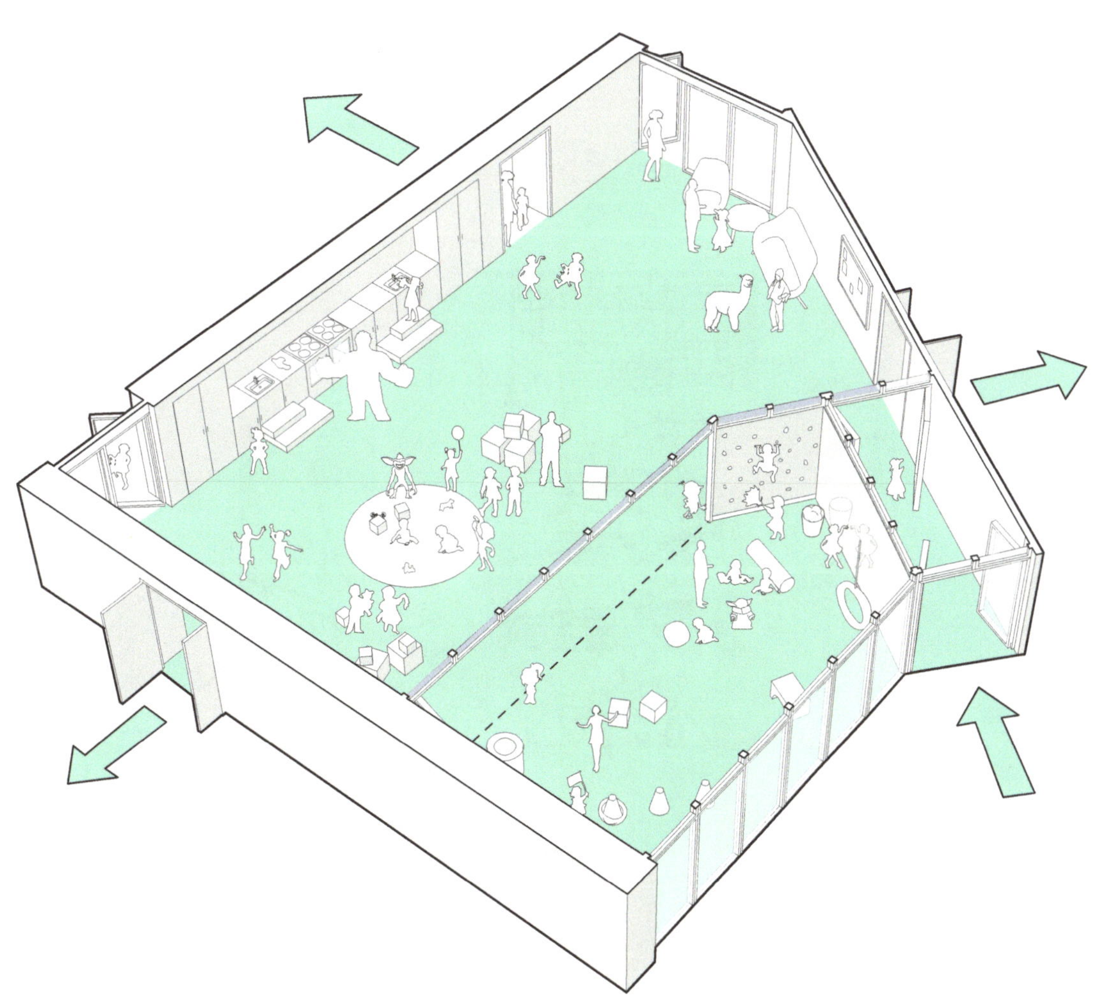

Use tracing paper

Baking paper, bumwad, trash paper...it goes by many names that do not do justice to how awesome this thing is. Think of it as a layer in photoshop...but in reality! You can sketch over an existing plan over and over, making it slightly more refined, or you can move some parts of the composition around freely. It also enables your drawings to communicate. Every new layer is an answer to questions posed by the previous.

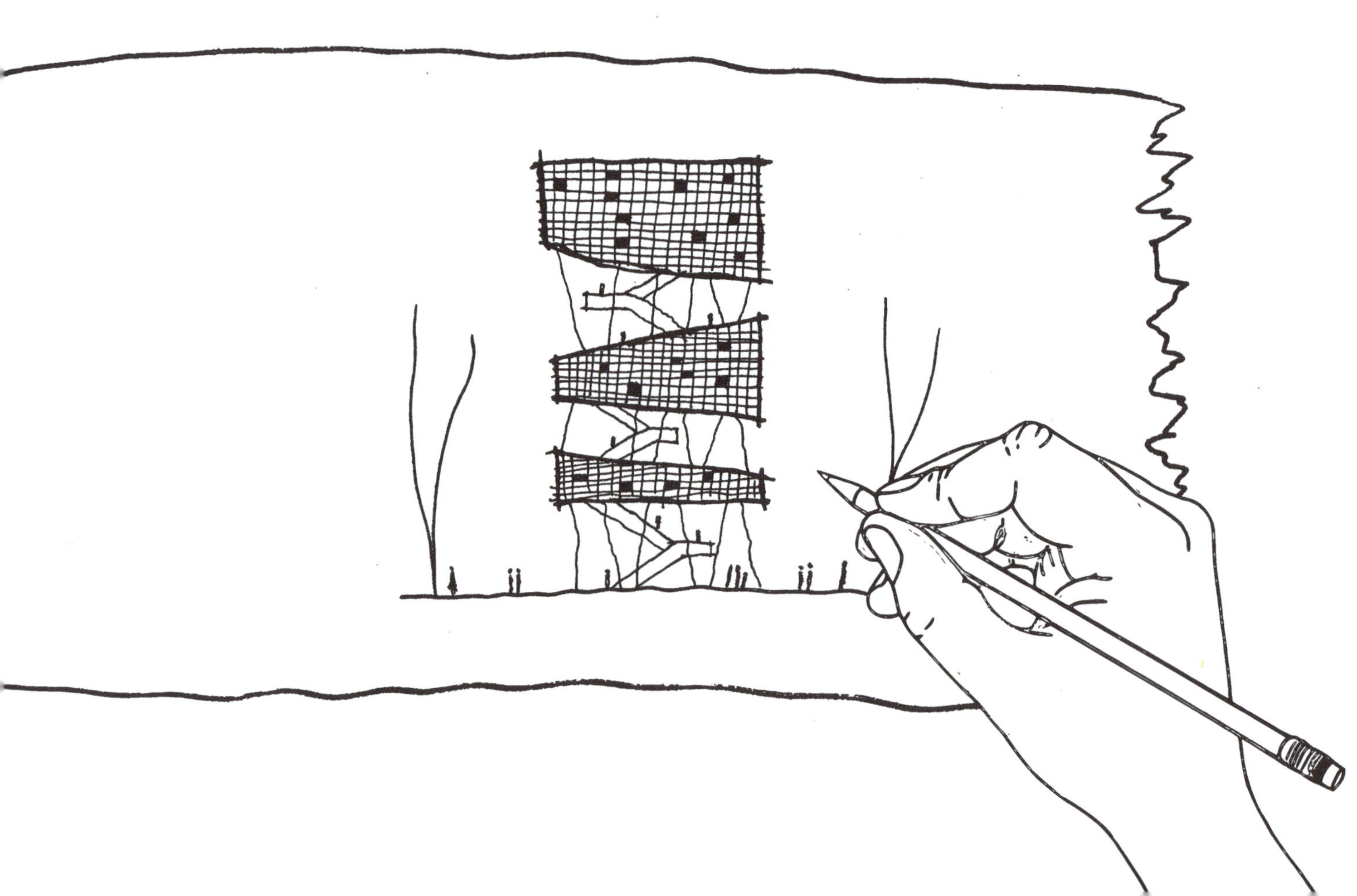

Objectivity vs. subjectivity

Two possible views of the same reality. Objective view is detached from it, carefully observes and critically evaluates. Subjective view involves being one with the reality, seeing it from the inside, feeling it. It is connected with emotions. Both are needed in order to create architecture that is both relevant and logical but also beautiful and tempting.

The government's paw

The main tools for regulating the building design are zoning and building regulations, fire requirements and energy demands.

Zoning influences the impact of the building on its surrounding, regulates the height and density.

Fire demands regulate materials that can be used for building as well as required protection in case of fire (sprinklers, width of doors and corridors or number of independent escape routes).

Energy demands dictate the maximum amount of energy that a building can use.

Narrative and truth duality of architecture

Architecture connects the worlds; physical and spiritual. The finished building should be genuine, in the sense of using the materials, expressing and addressing its functions and be safe to use. Above that, there is also the story we want to tell, the social context of the building and the idea that started it all.

Embrace the sketching even though you are not great at it

I know the pain really well. In fact, I am anxious about showing you my sketches in this book because I would like them to be much nicer and refined. However, the truth is, that the sketches do not have to be exceptionally refined. Sketching is a language, and if your sketches can transmit the message you want to send, they are good!

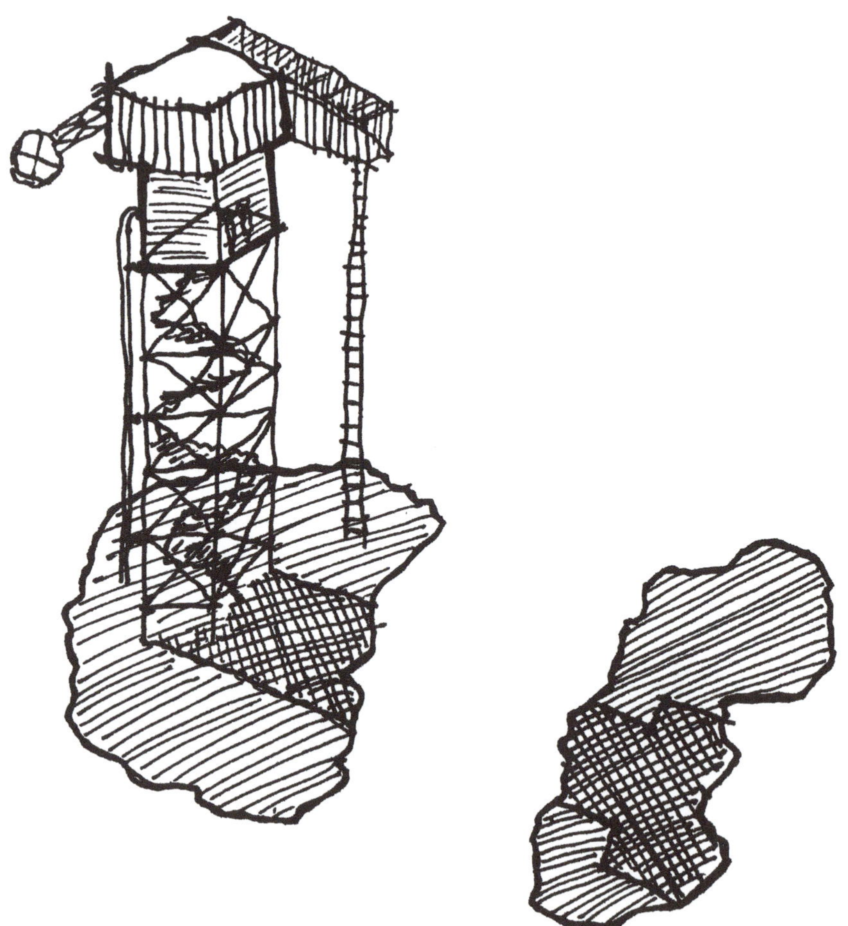

Be careful with colours

Architects only use black, white and shades of grey. That is one of the usual clichés that are being told about us. I know of two reasons for that. First of all, architecture is a stage for life, a framework for our being. And by making the colour palette subtle, you are leaving canvas blank for colourful presence of people, furniture and objects inside. Second reason might be that it is difficult to create the working palette with bright and saturated colours. Some architects and designers can do that and I admire them. Until I learn this dark magic myself, I intend to keep it subtle and let the materials do the talking.

Never place a door by the side of the bed

A great architect is also approximately 1/32 psychologist. One of the errors on a psychological level can be seen in many catalogue houses. The door to the bedroom right beside the bed. This will make the sleeping person uncomfortable since there might be potential threat entering the room.

It is preferred to locate the door in a clear sight from bed.

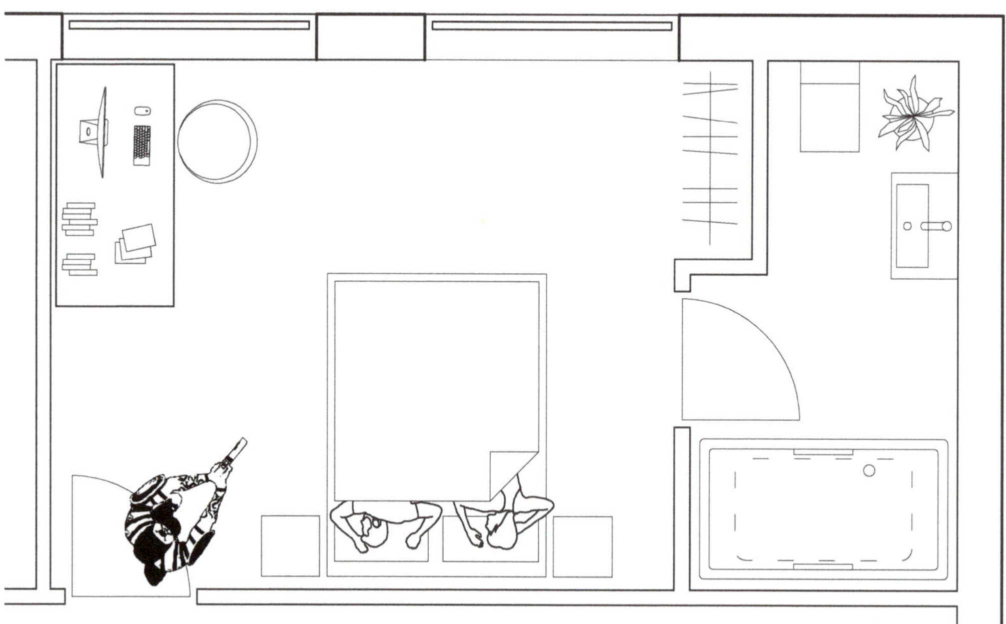

Create a routine

Everyone is different. However, most people are focused and productive in the morning. Use morning to do the most important task of the day and create a habit out of it. Habits are also great because you do not have to think about them and persuade yourself to do something, you just do it. Learn a thing or two about time management and personal motivation to boost your life.

EAT

SLEEP

WORK

ENJOY

REPEAT

Building complexity

One of the reasons it takes such a long time for an architect to make name for himself is the insane complexity involved in construction of buildings. The finished design solution must meet the building regulations, zoning, fire demands and energy requirements. At the same time it must keep the weather out and the heat in. On top of that, it should also feel comfortable and induce emotions in the users.

Making sure all of these work together requires wide range of expertise gained through continuous and never ending improvement.

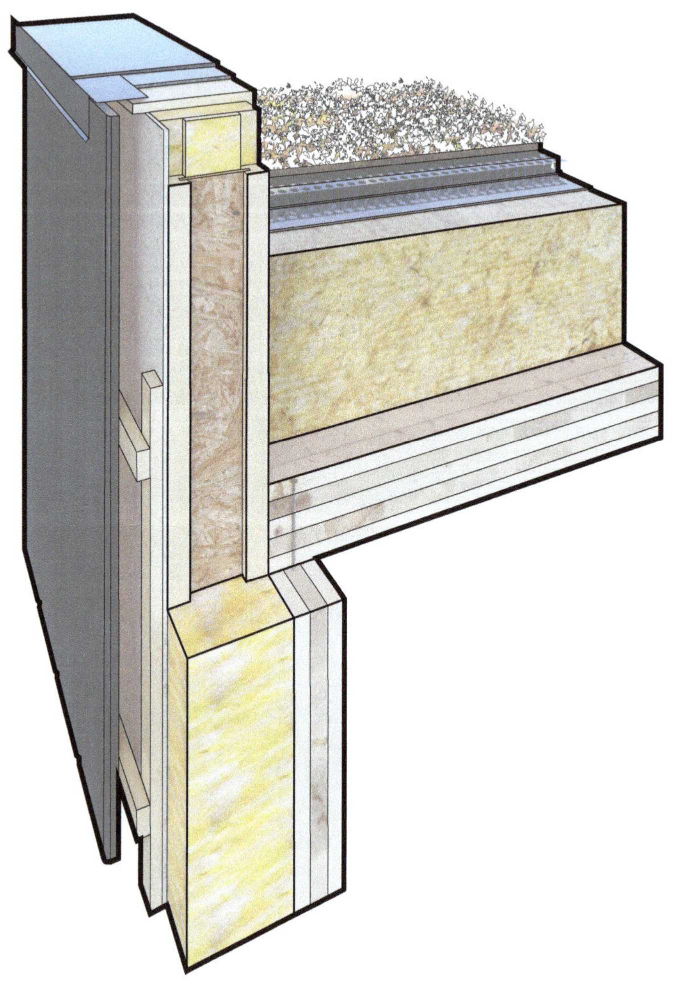

Find your own architecture

There are countless styles of architecture. Some architects believe that architecture arises from materials, other firmly follow the function. Some are proud of their engineering, other carefully consider the local context. None of them is wrong. Architecture is what you want it to be.

What do you want it to be?

Make sure important decisions are made by competent people

There are many parties involved in the building industry and many of them have tremendous impact on what is going to be built. For example city council actually has greater influence on what gets built than architects, but don't remind them.

Developers have vast financial resources that can be channelled towards making a better built environment for us. Our duty, as architects, is to educate and guide people who make decisions.

Volume to surface ratio

Even if two solids have the same volume, there can be a big difference in surface area.

The compact spaces are easier to heat because less energy escapes through the building envelope. On the other hand, be careful not to design boring cube just for the sake of energy efficiency.

Bigger surface area allows for greater variety of uses, provides more space for fenestration and is visually more interesting. All that at a cost of more energy used.

Sometimes you will have to choose one of the two extremes. Other times you can find a way to balance both.

Box 10x10x10 m	4 Boxes 5x5x10 m	8 Boxes 5x5x5 m
Volume 1000 m3	Volume 1000 m3	Volume 1000 m3
Surface area 600 m2	Surface area 850 m2	Surface area 1050 m2

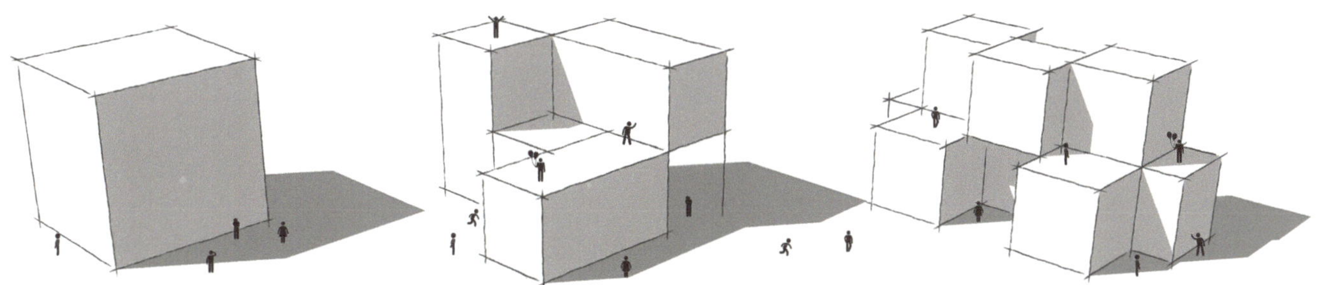

Making before managing

Architects often become who they are because they love to create. The catch is, that the older you get, the more things need to be managed. I know a great architect, who solved this conundrum by splitting his day in half. He wakes up early in the morning (4 AM) and creates. Drafts, models, plans. He leaves the studio before lunch to go hiking or cycling. That is an interlude to restart his mind. And after lunch, there is a time for managing. E-mails, phone calls, meetings, everything that needs his attention. It works for him and I really admire his way of living a creative life and setting priorities.

6AM | Making

11AM | Interlude

3PM | Managing

Architects make sure gravity works and water stays outside

Aside from aesthetics, the core task for an architect is to make a building that is safe to inhabit and its users are comfortable inside. Practical requirements and artistic quality must both be satisfied with equal importance.

The mistake some architects are making is that they focus too much on the artistic expression and do not know how to finish the building so it is convenient for occupants and long-lasting. On the opposite side of spectrum there is a mistake of inability to aspire to achieve greatness because of fear that the building will be too complex to construct.

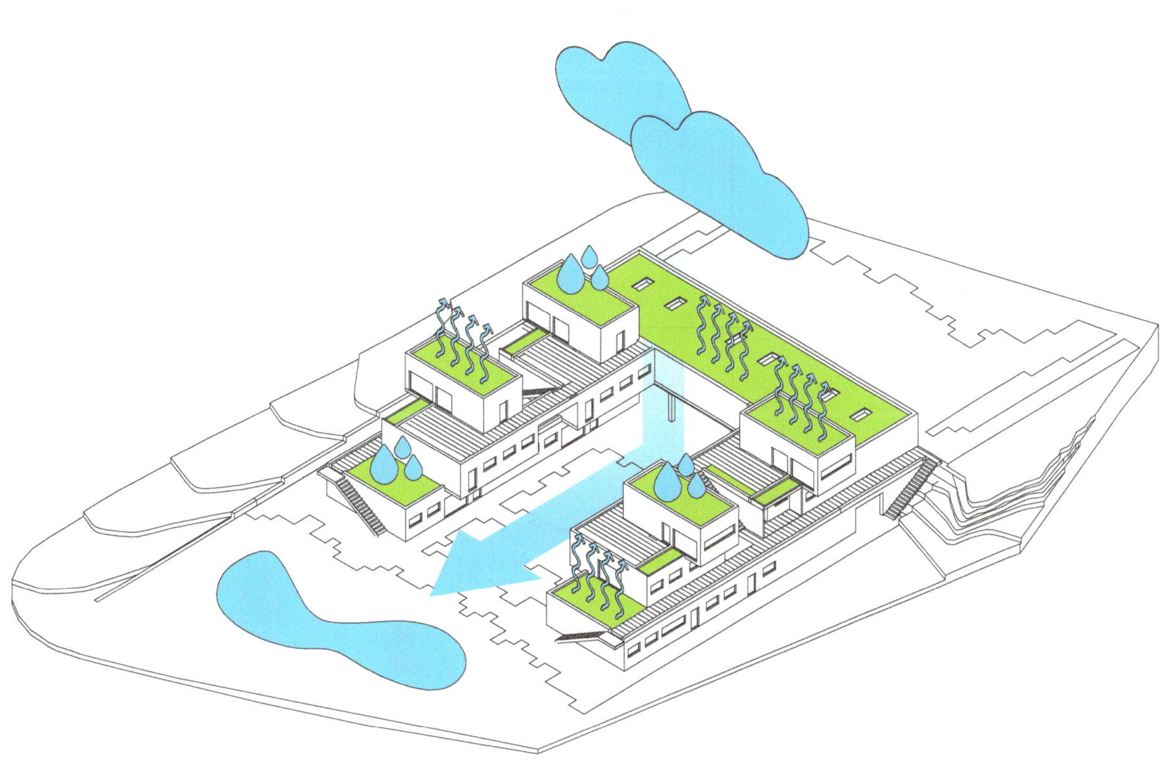

Sun is both friend and enemy

You can use the sun to passively heat the building in winter, however, be careful about overheating during the summer.

Sun illuminates spaces, yet it can also cause glare and disrupt work.

Elements that can control the passage of sun rays include, but are not limited to overhang, sunshade, awning, louvre, screen or brise soleil.

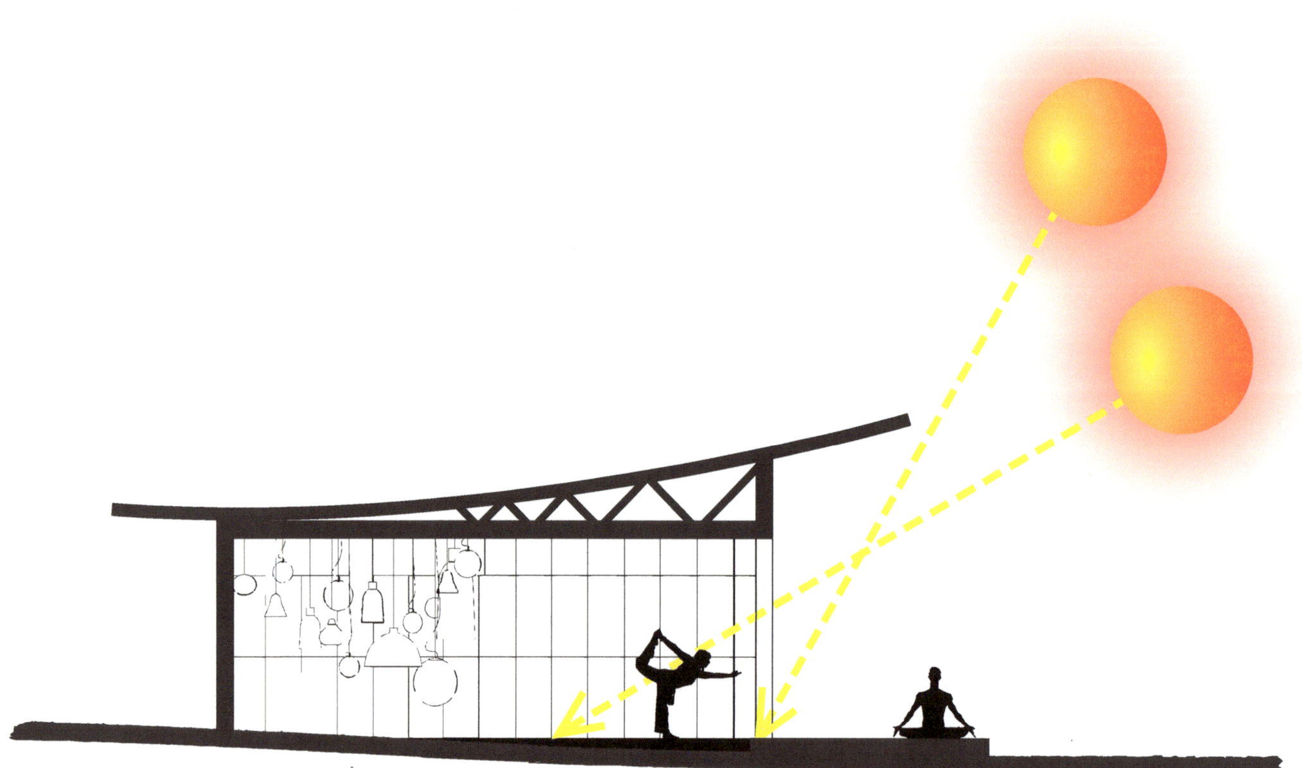

Be findable

Social media are big thing these days. Pick some of them and learn about marketing and building a personal brand. This will ensure that your work can be discovered by other people and your values shared with the world. You can connect with anyone around the world who is interested in the same ideas as you are. Create a synergy with those individuals and bring new things to the world.

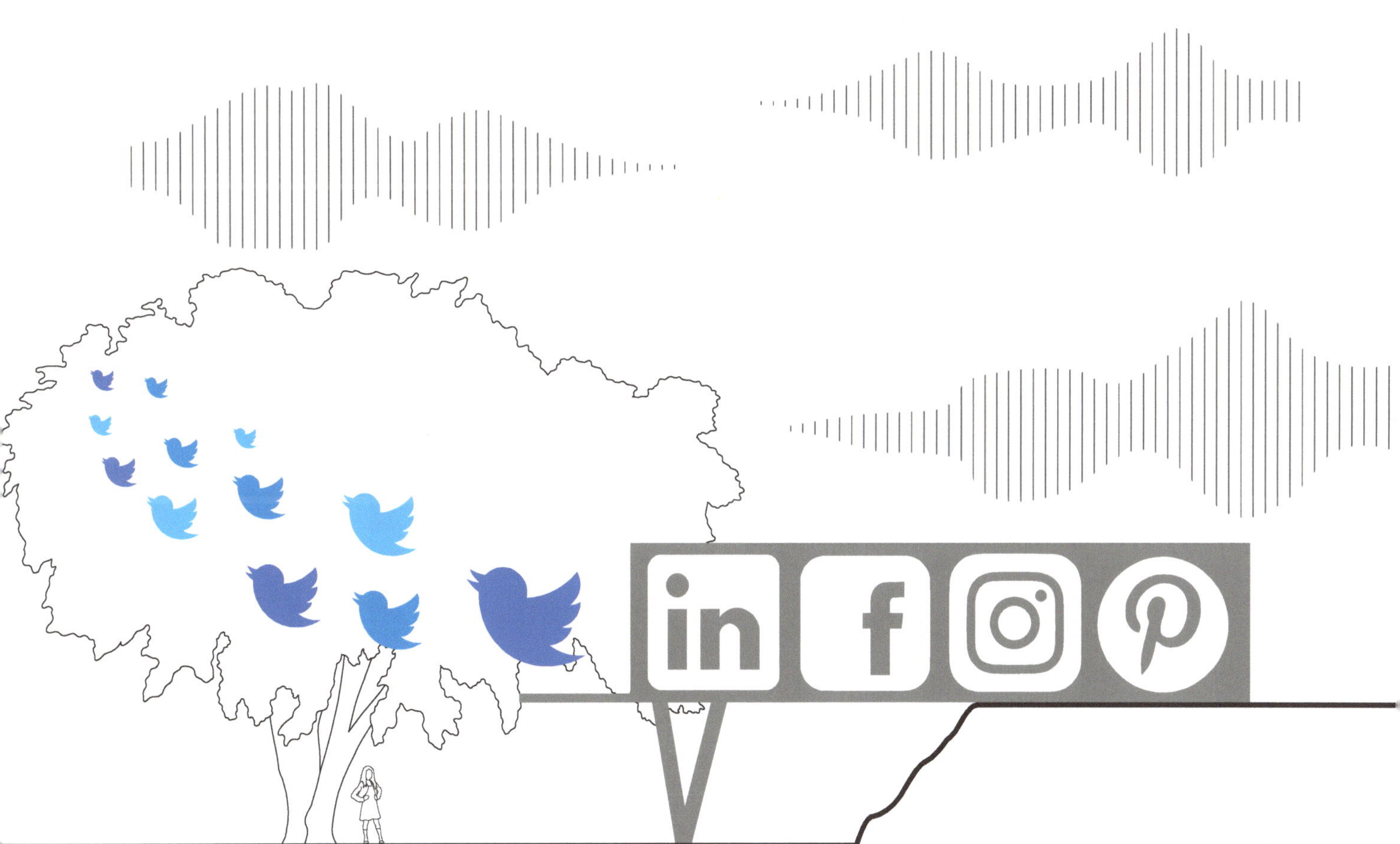

Symbolic meaning

As a society, we use many symbols to quickly assign a meaning without complicated description. Cross on the church or stick figure on the toilet doors are symbols.

In a similar manner, your design can become a symbol. Symbol for the city, symbol for the institution that occupies the building or symbol of the neighbourhood.

Let the site guide your design

For many architects, the building site is a major factor shaping the design. Study it carefully and note all the important constraints and possibilities. Topography, easements, views, sun path, prevailing winds, surroundings, access and more.

Some of these are critical constraints that will limit the area the building can be designed on. Others will guide you to locate the right spot for the building.

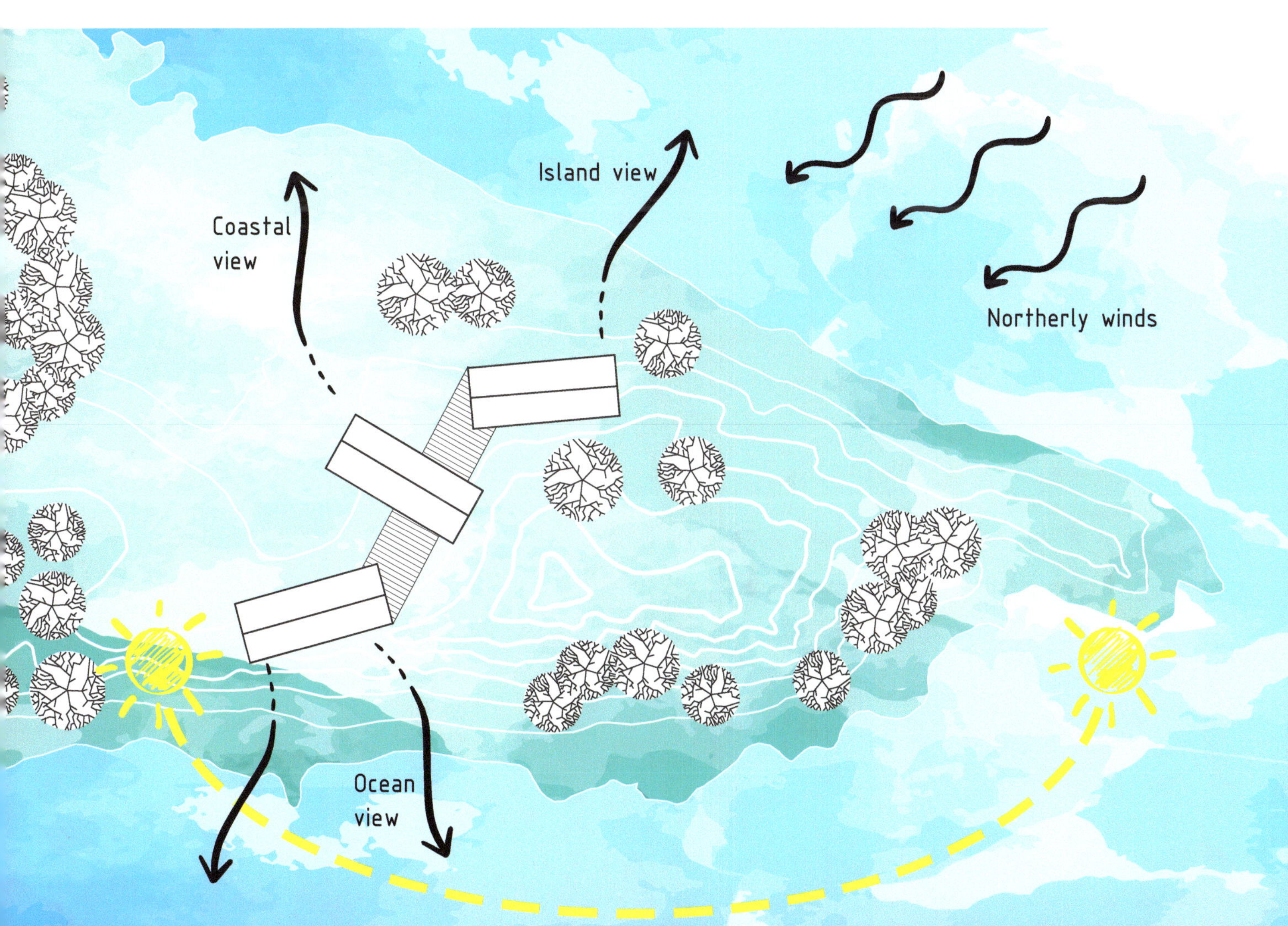

One diagram to bind everything together

A simple diagram is a great tool how to explain your concept. If one diagram is enough to fully understand a project, you did a great job and your design communicates itself.

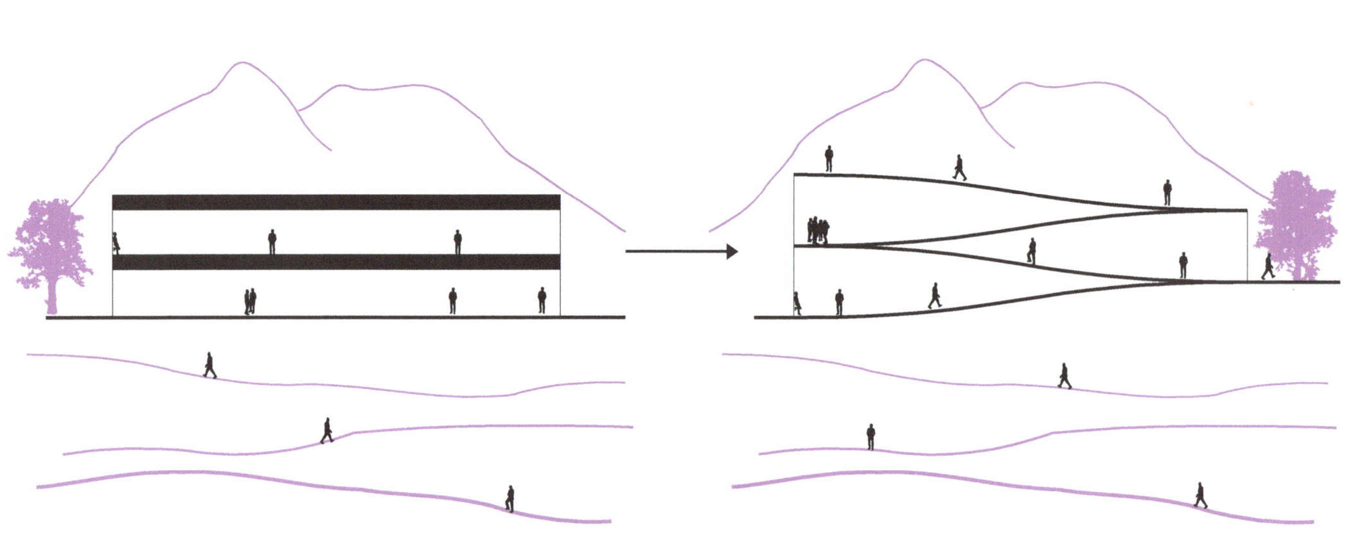

The true beauty

More than in each individual element, beauty lies in the composition. Holistic arrangement is more than just the sum of the parts. The interaction between the parts matter. Their proximity, their relative size, their orientation in space. Work carefully with chosen elements, because even the most interesting parts cannot save a poor composition.

Learn how to compose text and pictures on a sheet

Architects are great at making visually attractive presentations. Careful arrangement of images and written text is a crucial skill. Learn a thing or two about visual design, it will help you to make neat presentation boards and competition booklets.

Be a process oriented to create better result

Great result comes when you focus on the process. Try to understand problem before chasing after solution.

Ask yourself what could happen if. Always seek new ways to improve existing conditions. Accept the uncertainty that follows the design process. Accept that every decision might need to be changed in the future if it does not work. Make holistic decisions. Do not try to force decisions that do not work. Re-evaluate your decisions often throughout the project. Distance yourself from your work and allow yourself a critical point of view. Do not be afraid to throw away good ideas. Allow yourself to revive discarded ideas. Embrace the powerlessness of not knowing, it is only temporary.

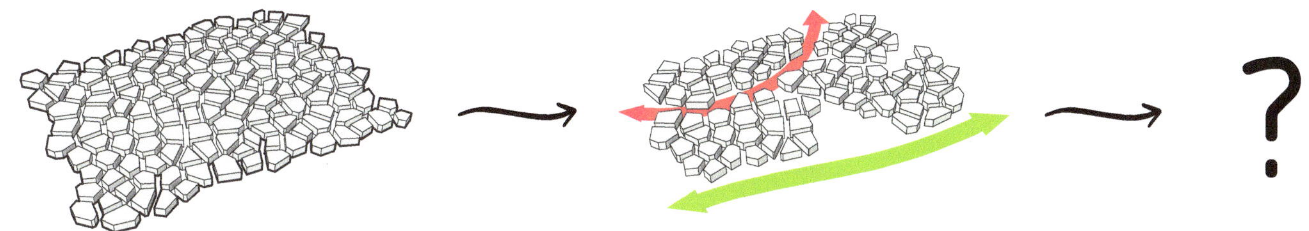

Take your time

At the time of writing, Bjarke Ingels is considered to be a young architect at the age of 45! What does that tell us? It takes a lot of patience and dedication to be an architect and it is a long-term investment. Many architects become known quite late in their life.

That is mostly because architecture as an industry is so complex. A great architect must know something about anthropology, history, sociology, psychology, materials, art, entrepreneurship, marketing, politics, physics, sales and many other fields.

The best thing you can take from a school project is not a perfect building but an improved process.

It is better to make some mistakes early, when they do not cost any money to make. That will change once you leave the protection of the academic bubble. Because of that, the most important goal is to grow as a designer and improve the way you operate on a daily basis. Create a strong work ethic and remember what worked and what did not. Transfer those skills into your professional life.

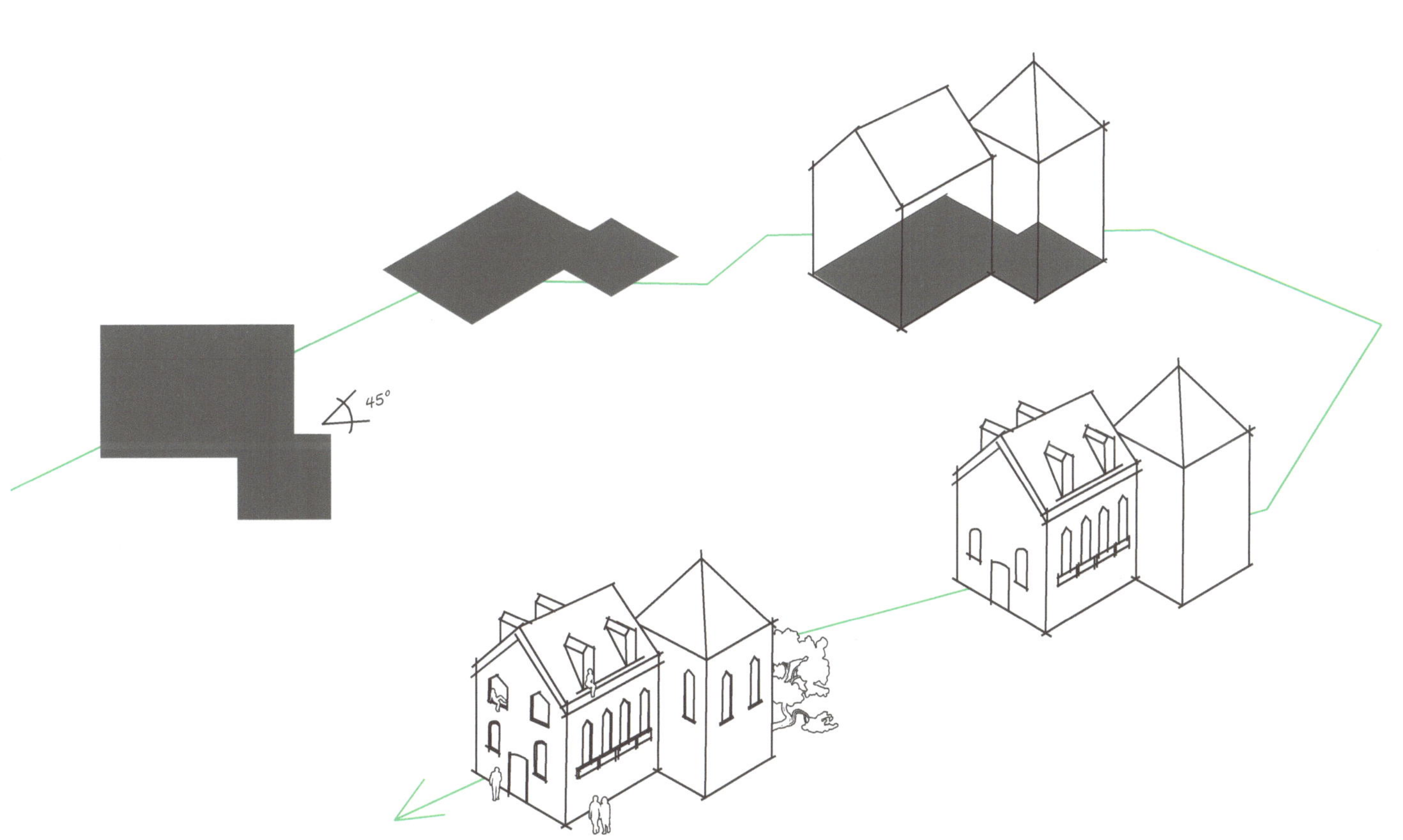

It is not a shame to discard a good idea

Not every idea suits every project. Be comfortable with letting go. Also, do not try to overload a project with too many ideas. It can look great in the beginning, however, it will fragment the impact of each individual idea and it can end in a chaotic dissonance. You can write your idea down and save it for later, its time will eventually come.

Name it

As soon as you have the idea, give it a name. Having a name in mind will help you to better understand what have you created. This applies both to the name of the initial form (pebble tower, tube pack, extruded corner) and to the name of the project as a finished product. There is nothing more boring than when your masterpiece is named 56 Leonard Street (sorry Jacques and Pierre).

Embrace the problem

Quite often, the problem is not something we can easily overcome and the best solution we come up with cannot simply erase it.

We can do the opposite, accept the problem and reiterate it. Maybe we have been dealt a bad hand, but we can switch a table and celebrate the constraints in front of us. It is exactly there, face-to-face with big problems, where great architecture is born.

Just do it

When it is too much for you, the most basic advice I can give you is to start. Right now. Take a pencil and start drawing, writing or making models. You will learn about the problem on the way.

Constraints fuel creativity

There is a common misconception that the best thing architect can get from a client is an unlimited budget and a big, flat site. That cannot be further from truth. Architect given this brief would probably go mad with so many possibilities. The best architecture comes from constraints. They can challenge you and force you to think outside the conventions. Steep site, limited budget, narrow site or noisy surrounding? All those can be overcome with grandiose. Turn the problem into an opportunity.

Read a lot

Not just your body, but the soul needs to be fed every day. Read about just anything you can get your hands on, technical brochures, design, architecture, visual arts. Read the news so you know the general direction of the society. Architecture is a field that is connected to the world and you should know a little bit about everything.

Sketch every day

I am so failing at this and I regret it often. Learn from my mistake and carry a sketchbook around. Be observant and sketch what you see during the day, scribble any idea that comes to your mind during the morning commute or quickly note that one spark of an idea that crossed your mind during the day.

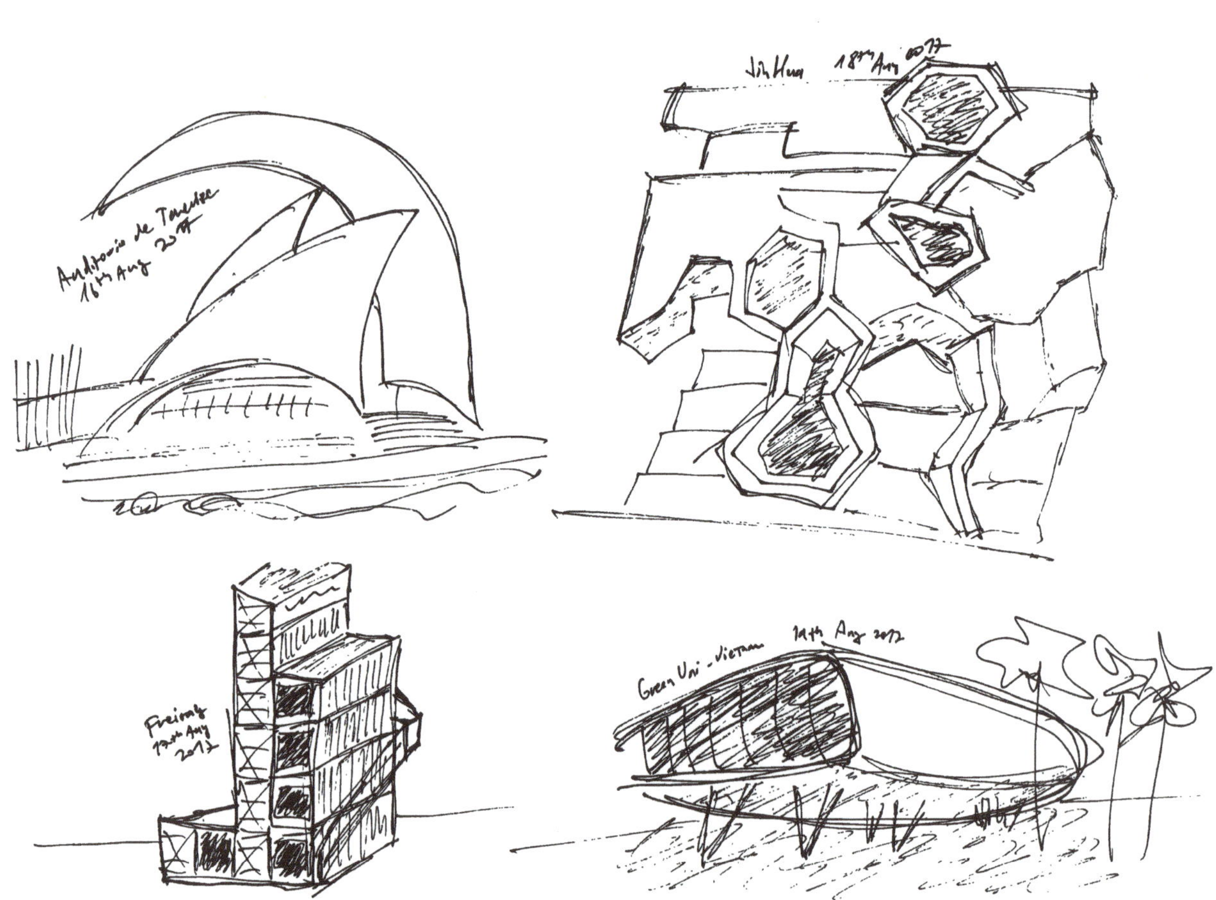

Learn from mistakes

Nobody said that the mistakes have to be yours though. Be observant and evaluate your moves and moves of the others. Why do some succeed and others fail? Find the common reasons why good ideas failed and be careful not to repeat the same mistakes. If you knew it happened before, it was not a mistake, it was your bad choice.

Pick a laptop with biggest screen possible or have a second monitor

Times, when architects spent hours at the drafting tables with ruler, triangle and protractor are long gone. Even though I encourage the use of "offline" tools as much as possible, you will still spend a considerable amount of time sitting at your desk. Make sure you have a proper posture and that your screen is big enough. Your eyes will thank you and you will also double your productivity.

Store your ideas for later

Not every idea is right for the project you are doing right now, but it might be for the next one. Make sure all of your ideas are in paper or digital form. Neither paper nor hard disc forget, your brain might. Archive everything.

Be eloquent speaker

Learn some fancy words, do not try to impress others with them though. May seem contradictory, I know.

I believe that it is always great to expand your vocabulary and use some words that are not traditional. Just do not learn them for the sake of making people impressed, you will look pretentious and others won't open up to you since they do not want to sound less intelligent.

Sophisticated asymmetry

Generally speaking, it is hard to achieve balanced asymmetric composition. Therefore, if properly executed, it is held in high regard. Symmetric compositions are balanced on their own and therefore easier to achieve. They are a safe bet, however, they might sometimes be considered boring.

Asymmetry allows more possibilities to locate the programme inside, since it permits greater degree of freedom.

Asymmetry

Symmetry

Stay up to date with current software

Trends are moving so fast that it is hard to keep up.

That is no excuse, though. You do not have to know every single piece of software, but keep your brain sharp and work with new and emerging tools so you can pick-up the one you might need quickly when the requirement arises.

Zoom in-zoom out

The building should be equally well-thought-out in micro and macro scale. Both its relationship to the city, a doorknob and everything in-between is important.

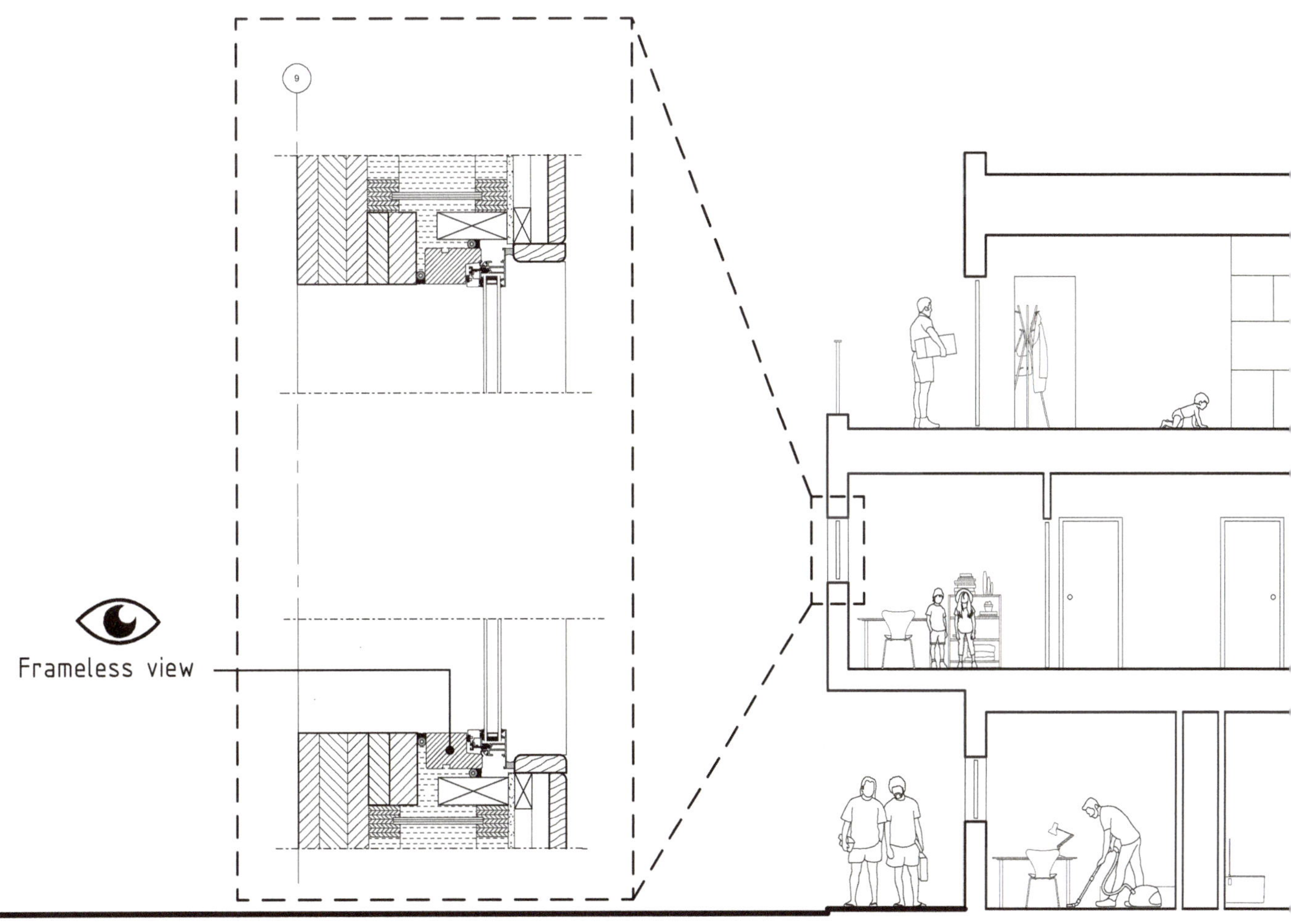

Ask for feedback - friends or foes

Even though you have to swallow your pride first, it is great to have someone else to look at your work. Let them criticize it, even ask them to do so. When you work on something for a long time, you get blind to the obvious and you get emotionally attached to your work. It might sometimes be hard to hear different opinions, but it is worth it. That is how the best ideas come to life when people argue and try to triumph over each other with better and better idea.

What does a shape imply?

Different shapes convey different message to the user. Square is static and has no inherent direction pattern, whereas rectangle has longer and shorter sides. Because of that it is more dynamic and promotes circulation through its longer axis. Circle faces no direction and is impossible to say where is the front or back. Think of what directional qualities other shapes have. Crescent, triangle, semi-circle or polygons.

Circulation in small rooms

The best option for circulation through a small room is close to the wall on a shorter axis, in that way, the user of the room will not be interrupted by people passing through.

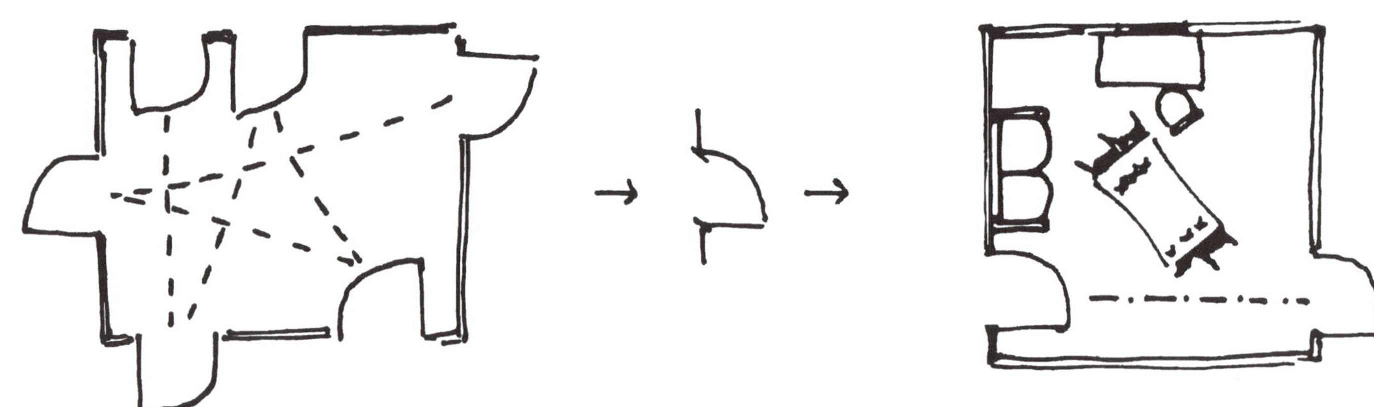

Different types of windows serve different means

Small carefully placed window can frame the particular view to an interesting object outside. Wall of glass distorts the boundary between inside and outside.

Clerestory windows allow deep penetration of light into the building and deny unwanted views inside.

Set below the knee level, windows create a dynamic shift of focus and illuminate the path.

Skylights provide high amount of even illumination from above.

Make sure it is what you want it to be

When you have a particular interest in a quality of an element, make sure the quality is really there. If the space should feel high, it really must be high. If the space should bathe in light, ensure there are openings facing the right direction. If you want the walls to feel light, make sure they are not from bricks. Experienced designers can make the same impact using much smaller means.

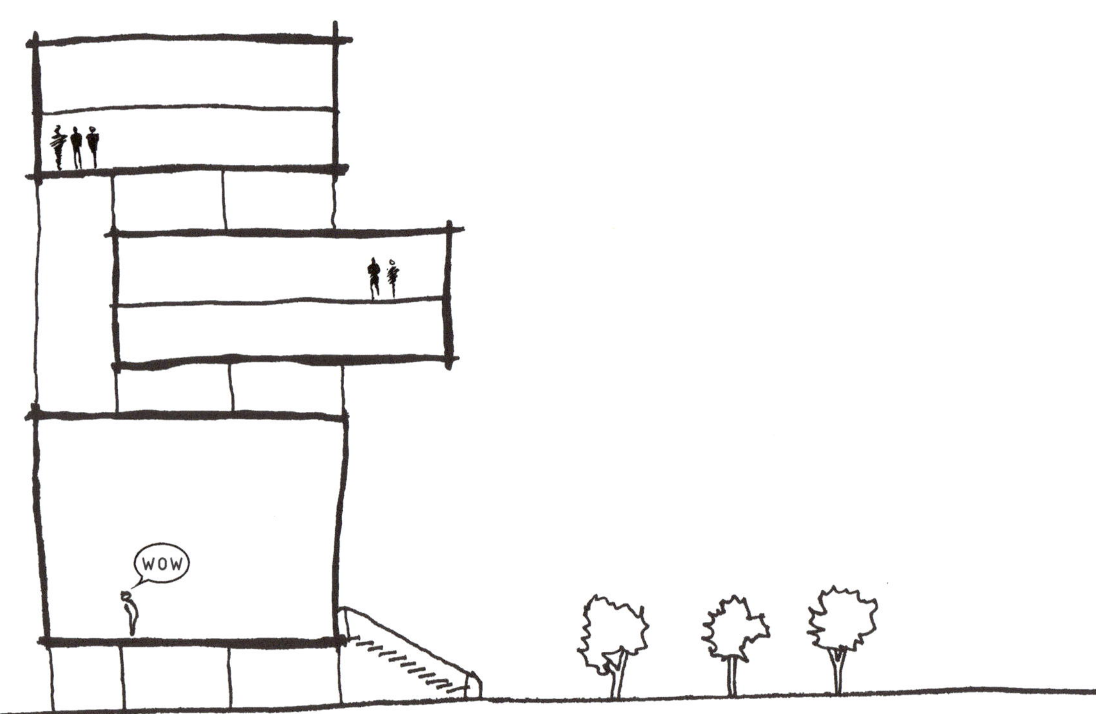

Create your own home office

Do you have enough space on the table? It is important to have all the tools you use at hand. And the literature for inspiration in a bookcase nearby. Make your space personal. Fill it with the things you like. You are your office. I also like to make a clear division between digital and analogue. Therefore I have two tables. One with a computer and one with pens, pencils, pastels, watercolours, LEGO bricks and rulers. That way, I am well aware when I am spending too much time looking at the screen.

Metacognition

Interesting and to some extent also frightening is when you think about how you think. Stop for a moment and realize your own thoughts.

Most of the day we work on an autopilot. We have breakfast, get dressed, lock the doors, commute to work or school. We do not think, we follow our habits. But when it comes to design, try to use meta-thinking to guide you through. Be aware of why are you making the decisions and how do you plan to implement them.

Redline your drawings

The practice of going through your own drawings and marking the mistakes or things that can be improved is a great exercise. There is always something missing, notes misaligned or the texture might look good on screen but not as good in print. You can also ask your colleagues to help you, but always do the first round yourself, so they do not have to pinpoint every minor mistake.

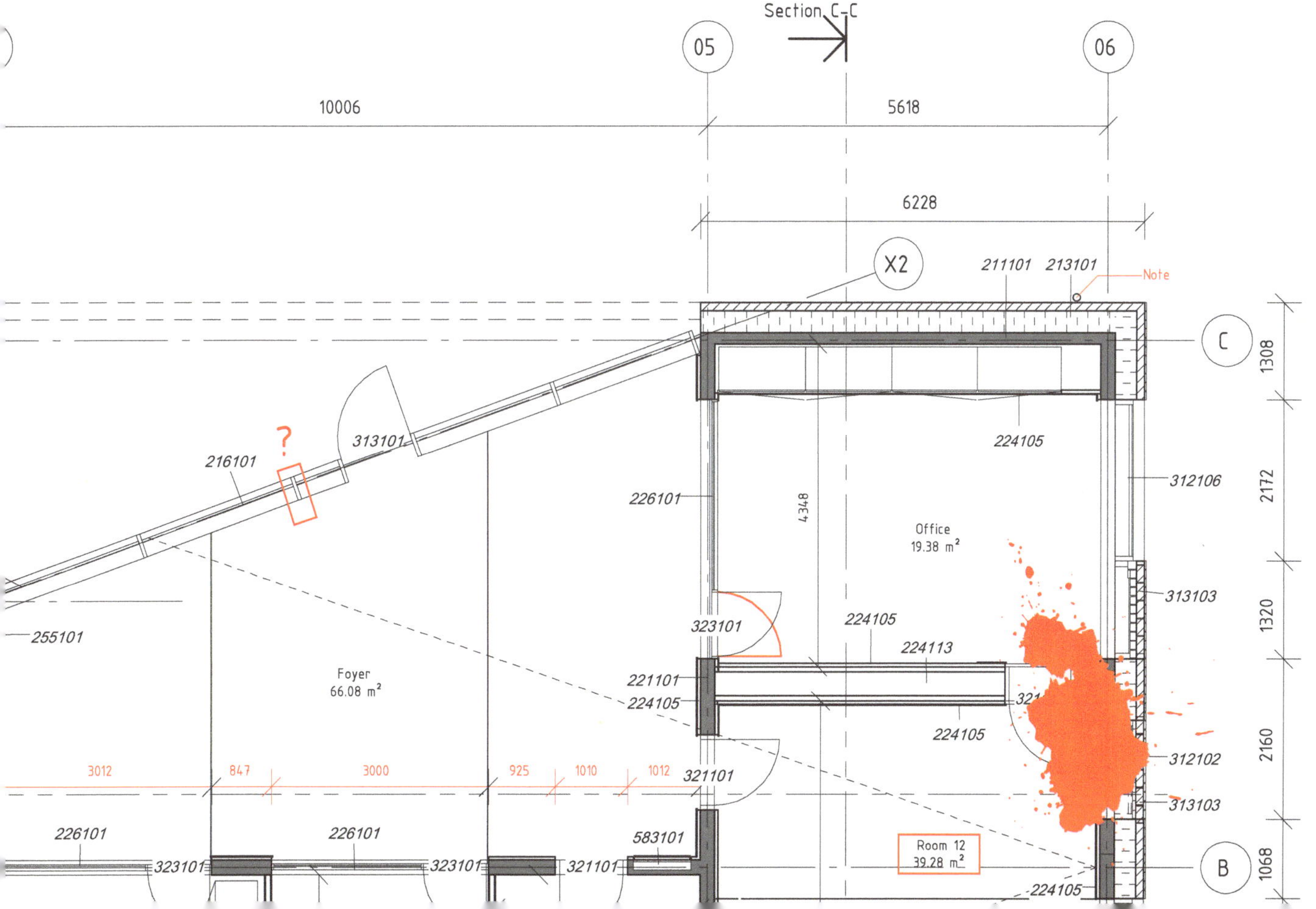

Should I stay or should I go

Thousands of years ago, we were used to moving through forests and dwell in caves and hill forts. This is still deeply embedded in our nature. And even though there is much less danger in current world, we still move through negative spaces because they remind us of a dangerous forest and we dwell in positive spaces because they are a safe haven. Keep that in mind when you want to create a space people will feel comfortable in.

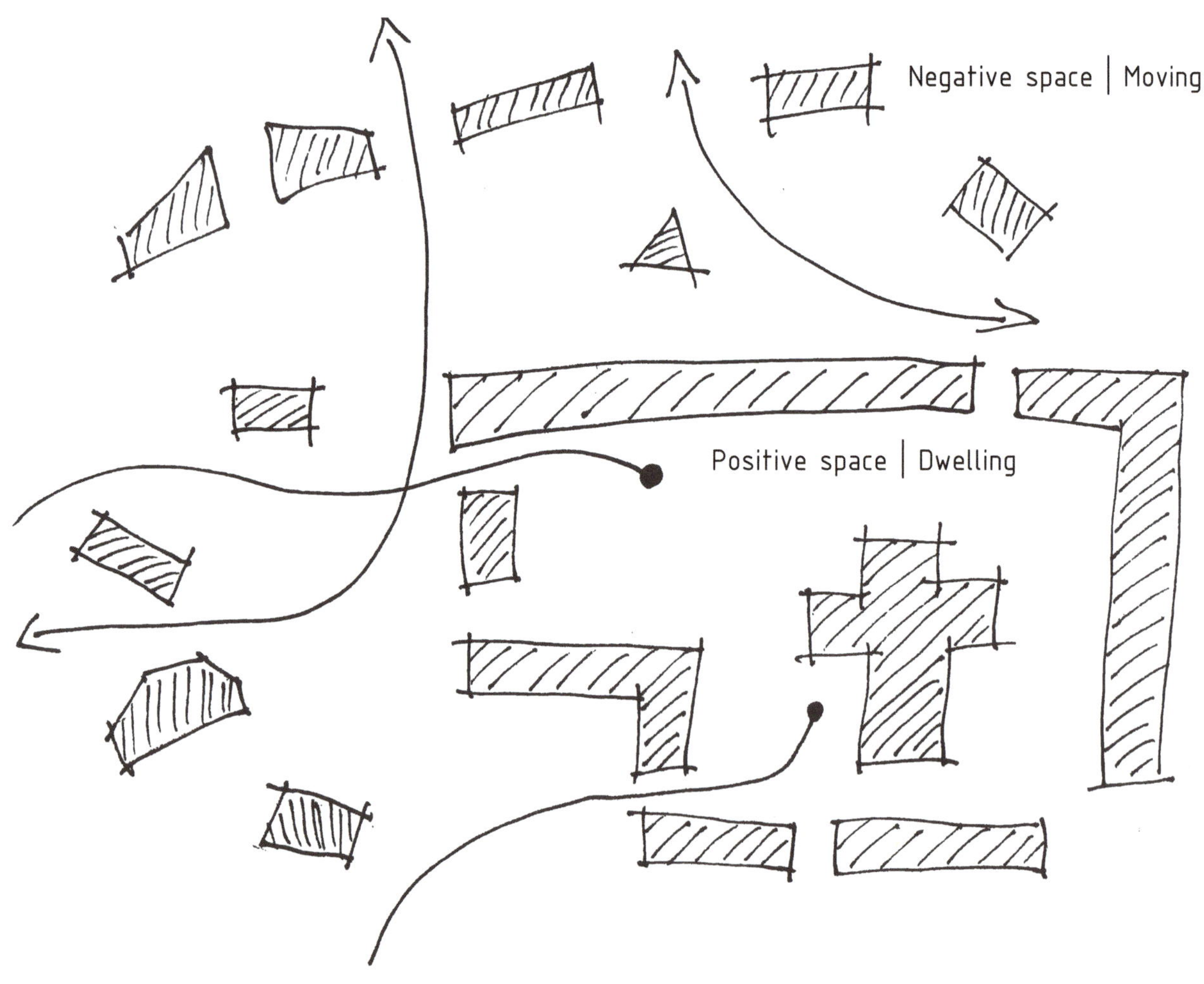

Vision of things yet to come

This advice applies to life in general. Always have a plan. For next week, month, year and beyond. Think of where you want to be in order to carve your own path. Never let others to decide on your behalf. Change your circumstances, not yourself.

The call of the solid

Voids and solids are three-dimensional counterparts to figure–ground theory. Voids are the absence of solid, or in other words "what is not". Solids are "what is". Together they create a three-dimensional composition. Use voids and solids in the early stages of design. They can intersect, add, subtract, merge, nest, puncture and perform other spatial operations.

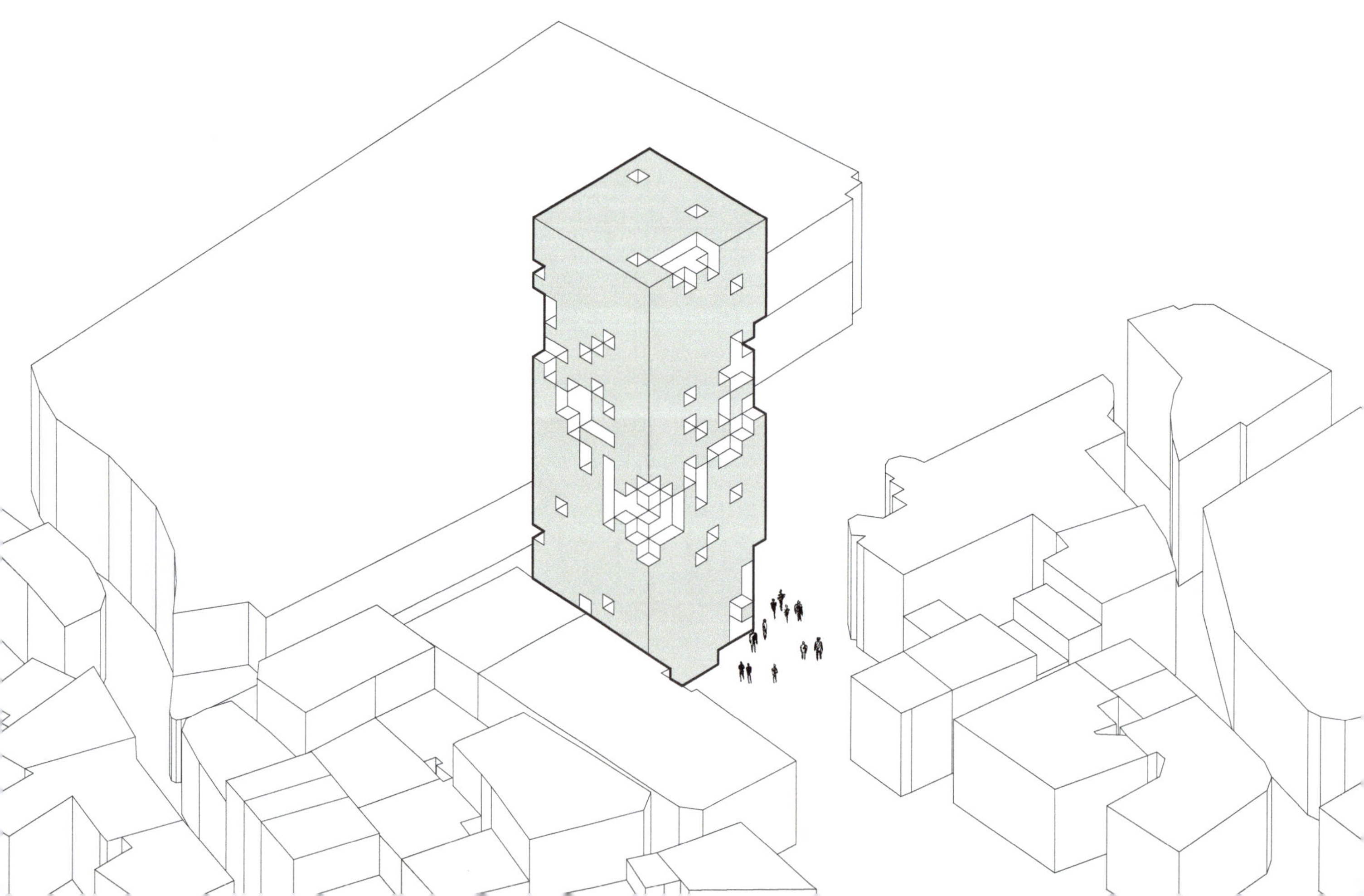

Good architecture tells a story

Humans are learning through stories. We are social creatures and we are hard-wired to listen. When we tell stories that have helped us shape our thinking and way of life, we can have the same effect on the others too.

Same applies to architecture. We see the world in a certain way. And through architecture, we can share our view. What should the world look like? Great architecture can carry a story through time.

Urbanism 101

Buildings in the urban environment create positive spaces. They closely interact with each other. They should blend in with the fabric of the city and create variety of lively spaces around; plazas, squares, promenades and such. Suburban buildings are free-standing. They do not have to conform, however, they also create negative space. You might live in the suburbs but you meet in the city.

New York | Urban

Moscow | Suburban

Have your own style

Consistency creates trust. If you want to build your personal brand or company use the same font, colour palette, paper type.

Same with your architecture. Over time, you will find out what makes you tick. What is your own style of design? If I get Frank Gehry to design my building, I will get a sculptural masterpiece. If I get Peter Zumthor, I will get humble, yet powerful building embedded strongly in its surroundings. If I get Bjarke Ingels, I will get a daring, non-conventional idea. What will I get when I hire you?

Gravity always wins

Every year buildings are more and more daring. Engineers are coming with new and exciting ideas on how to make our building taller, cantilevers longer and components stronger. There might come the time when the reign of gravity over design ends, however, I humbly assume that by that time both you and I will be having our eternal rest.

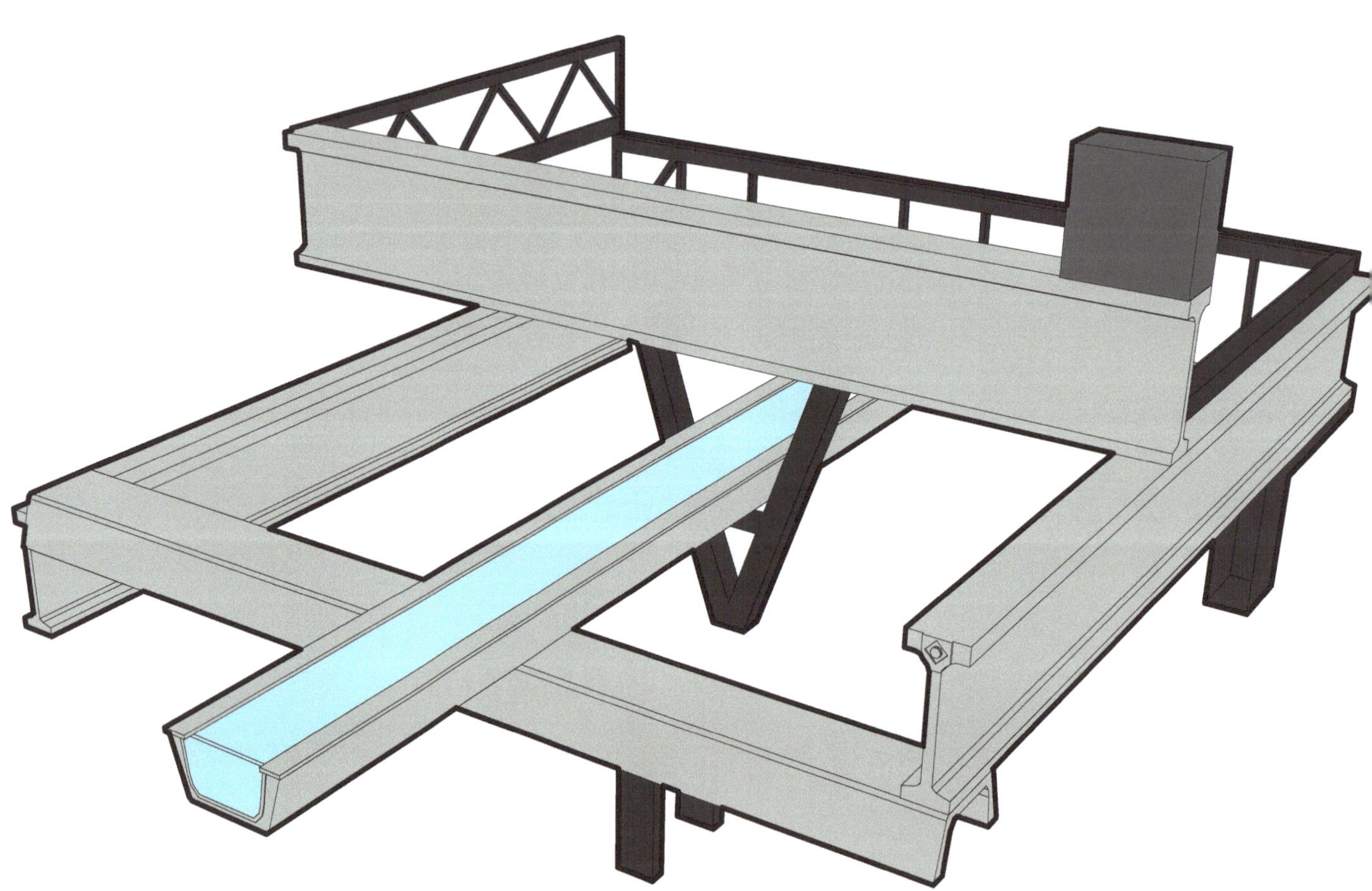

Hemeroscopium house | Structural diagram

Aesthetics of the building tell us when and where was it build

Different periods are characterised by different design approaches. In the past, buildings were limited by the structural properties of the building components. Different epochs fought the battle against gravity in different ways.

Different places had different influence on built environment. Climate, empires, culture, natural resources. All these factors are reflected in the architecture. What factors are shaping the architectural design now?

Lion gate | Greece

Tora gate | Japan

Villa Savoye | 1931

Disney Concert Hall | 2003

Presentation sequence proposal

- State the requirements and constraints

- Present core values

- Describe the process, discoveries and obstacles along the way

- Uncover the parti and show it on a diagram

- Present specific drawings and describe them in relation to the parti

- Follow with few specifics that address the microscale

- End up with critical evaluation of your work

Addition, subtraction, moulded

Most architectural forms can be simplified to:

Addition - assembly from smaller parts

Subtraction - cut away from larger part

Moulded - plastic material deformed by force

Abstract - everything else of uncertain origin

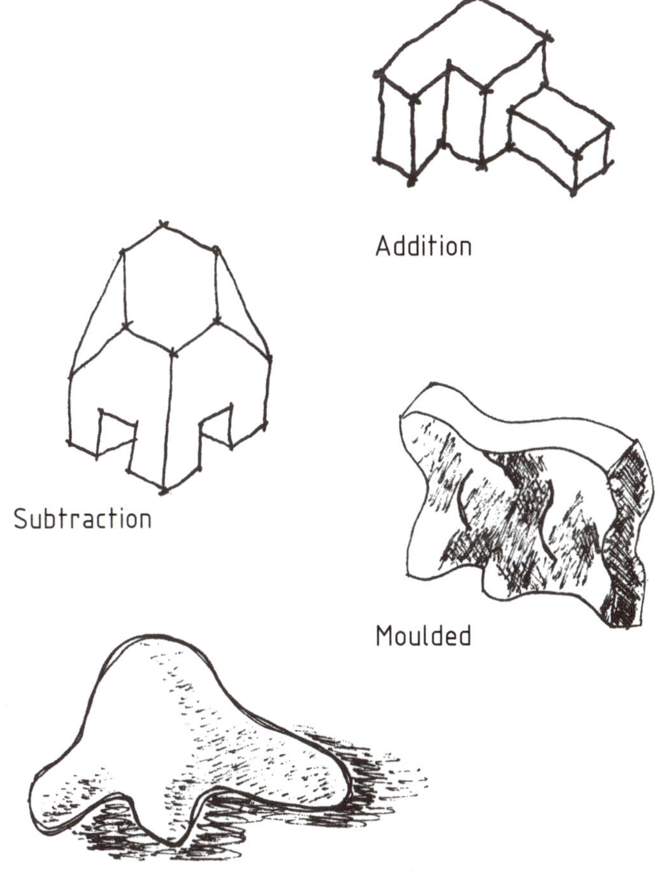

Addition

Subtraction

Moulded

Moulded

The Wave | Addition of moulded forms

The Iceberg | Subtraction from blocks

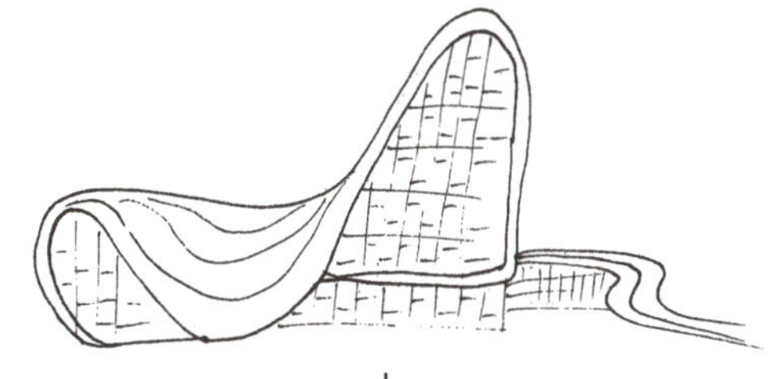

Heydar Aliyev Center | Moulded form

Know the materials

Materials are the body of architecture. Learn when and why to use one or another. What happens when you combine them? Wood and concrete go great together. Or you might want to just use one material in a flawless and unusual way. There are many different ways how one material can look. Concrete? Smooth, board formed from rough cut planks or with exposed aggregate? Wood? Treated, untreated, rough sawn, charred or weathered?

Walls through times

In the past, buildings had thick load-bearing walls that supported everything on top of them. This limited the building height and offered only rigid layout of interior. It was also costly and the higher the building, the thicker the walls had to be.

Nowadays, it is very common to have thin non-structural wall or curtain wall, that only forms a boundary between inside and outside. Those walls are hanging from the load-bearing structure that might be made of concrete or steel frame. This configuration also creates flexible interior spaces suitable for the ever-changing nature of human interactions.

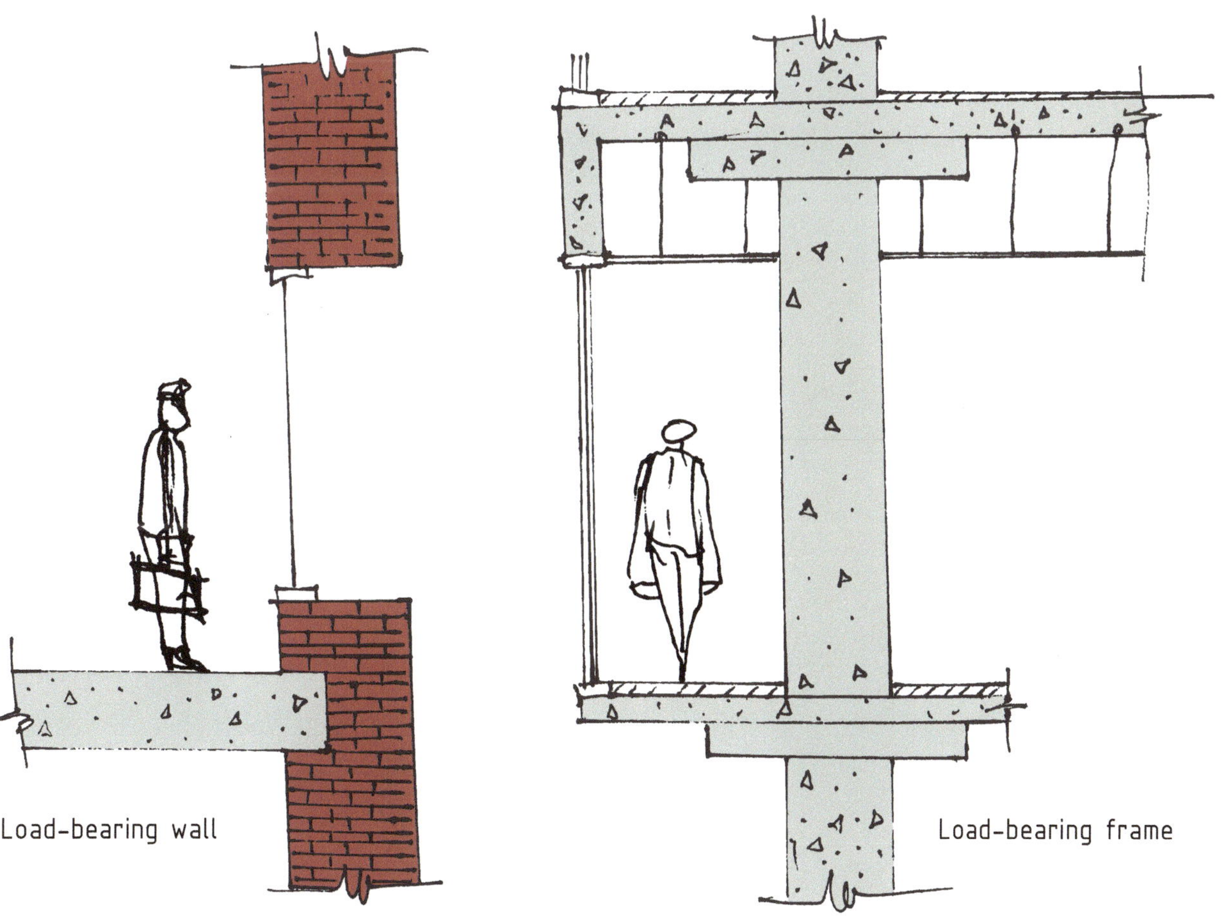

No building is an island on its own

The context of the surroundings is a vital part of the design. When on site, look around, listen and feel. What can fill the space in a harmonious way? How are people moving around and about? What can be seen from the site and how is the site seen?

In the natural context, how will the building react to the landscape around? Hills, lakes, forests?

Be perceptive, building is always part of the world.

Engineers are specific and architects abstract

Engineers are very exact people, concerned with details, specifics and numbers. They look at the world quantitatively. They measure and calculate what needs to be done.

Architects, on the other hand, are more concerned about relationships and abstract qualities, which might not be visible on the first sight. They are concerned with quality. They observe and link factors influencing design.

In the end, both are needed to create an architecture. They complement each other.

Control of process

The creative process is unpredictable. It feels anxious to admit we do not know where are we going. We have the responsibility for the project and it is unsure what lies ahead of us. We thought we have mastered the art of design when suddenly unforeseen circumstances erode the whole idea.

We love the process; sketching, making models, choosing materials, drafting, preparing presentations. However, with all this, anxiety comes, too. Is this the best we could do? Will they understand? Are they going to see the possibilities we see? Student or professional, those feelings can come to anyone and we have to live with them.

Served, servant, circulation

According to the theory of Louis Kahn, we can divide space into two categories, served and servant. The former are the main or primary areas such as living rooms, gallery spaces, auditoriums, classes, concert halls or offices, the latter are secondary areas such as technical rooms, storages, toilets or ventilation shafts. Their role is to support the primary places, they will be visited only briefly or by internal staff.

Originally, circulation areas were considered servant spaces as well, however, I would suggest thinking of them as a third category.

Diagram

First floor

Esherick house

Ground floor

The conductor of an orchestra

Architects know something about everything. It is their duty to settle arguments between different parties. Many people with different interests are involved in a construction of a single building. Architect is there to guide them all towards a successful finish.

In the ideal case scenario, everyone wins. The client is satisfied, workers got paid and contractors made profit.

Base-shaft-capital

Those are three parts of a column in an ancient Greece.

Buildings often follow this scheme. Supporting base, main part in the middle and decorated top that shows the significance.

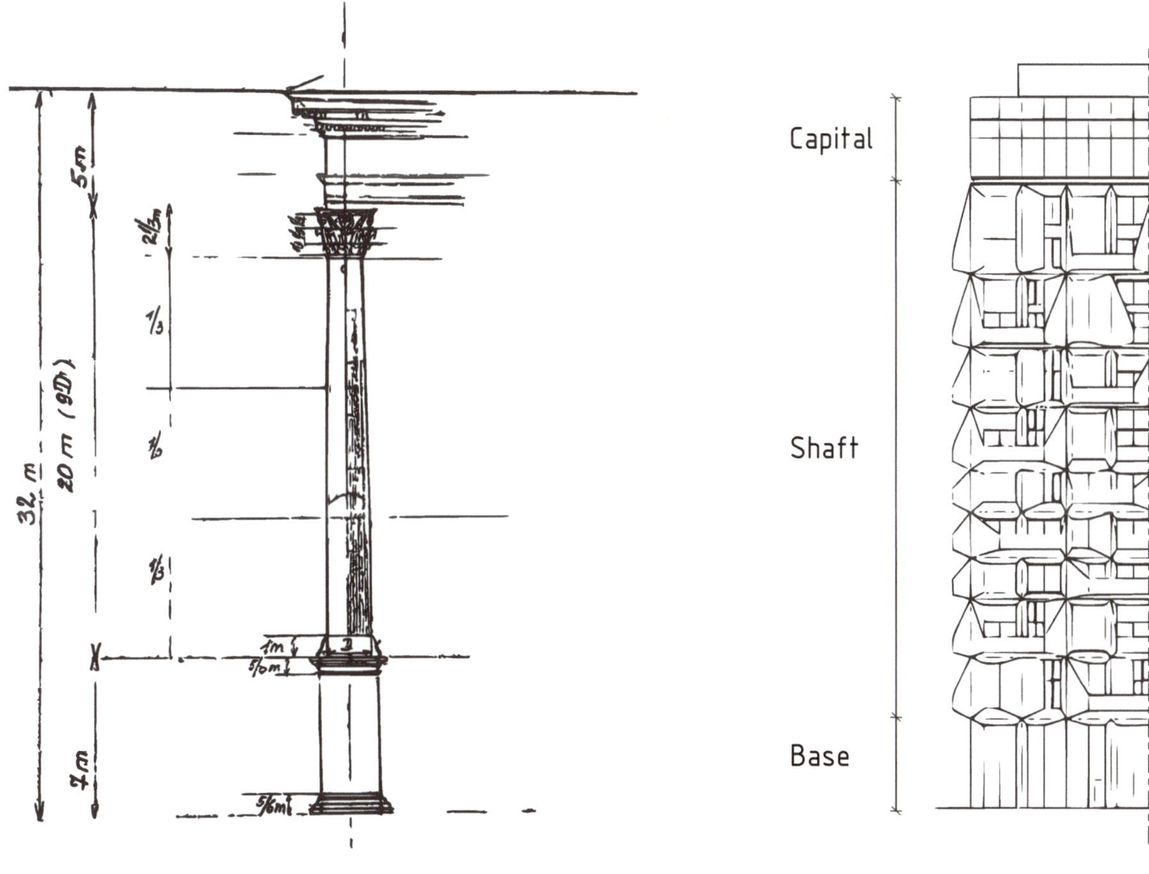

Qualities associated with materials

Concrete – cold, imposing, raw

Wood – warm, friendly, natural

Brick – humble, human-scale, unpretentious

Steel – light, crisp, firm

Glass – ethereal, fragile

Stone - sturdy, unyielding

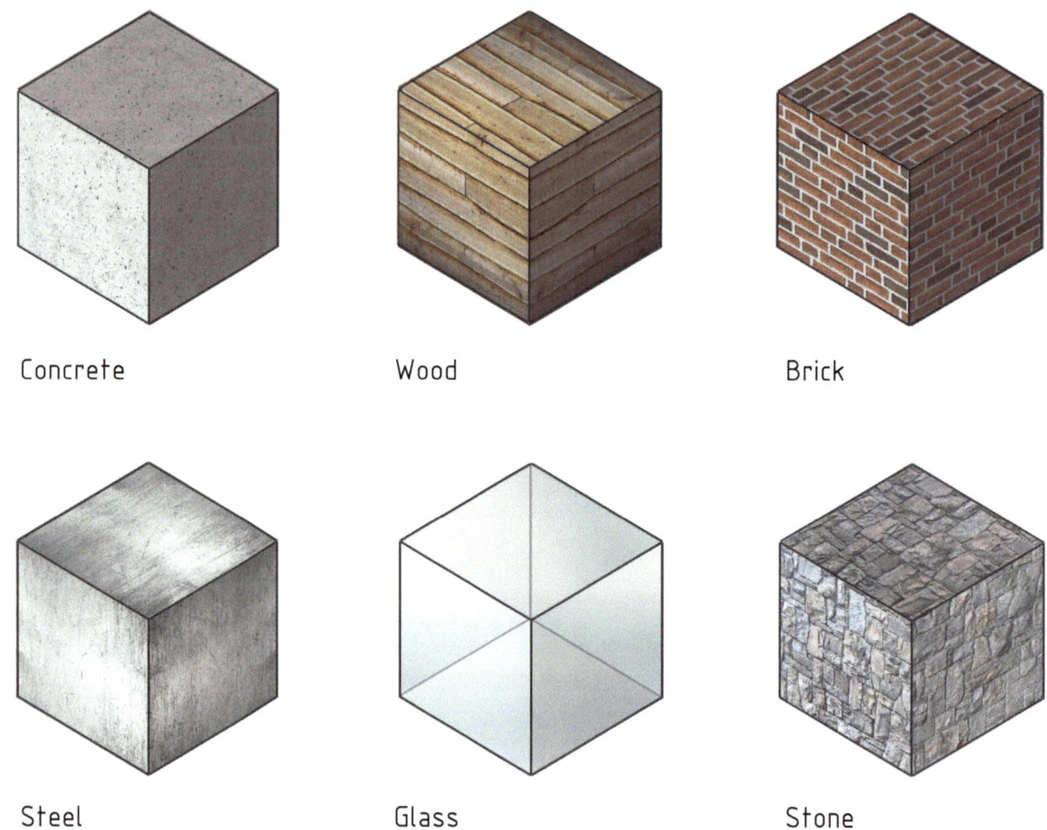

Concrete

Wood

Brick

Steel

Glass

Stone

Aim for the stars and you might land on the moon

There is nothing wrong with having big dreams and expectations.

Even though you might not reach them, it is better to closely miss than to achieve a mediocre goal.

Populate your drawings

People, furniture, trees and other minor objects on your visualizations are called entourage. They add a spark of life to your drawings and provide context. By making the drawings more attractive and relatable to the client, they increase the sales value of the whole presentation.

Section-plan dependence

Both types of drawings are inseparable from each other. Changes in one inherently influence the other. Design often starts with a plan, however, some building typologies or steep sites encourage to rather start designing with a section. If you start with plan or section does not matter, you will have to go back and forth until both work together.

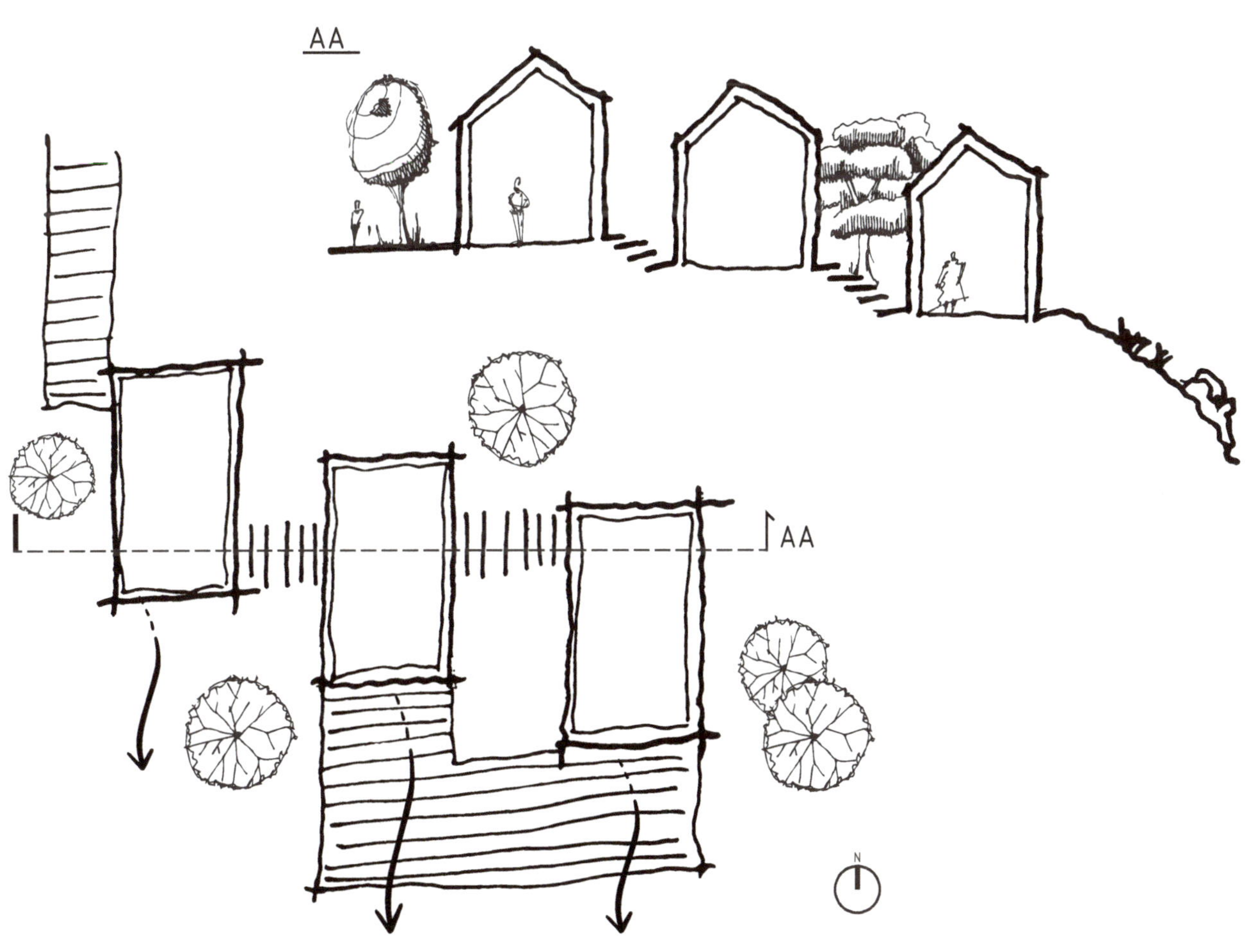

Use columns

They are not mere structural elements. They can enhance the material palette, demarcate the space, act as a gathering point or create a rhythmic colonnade.

  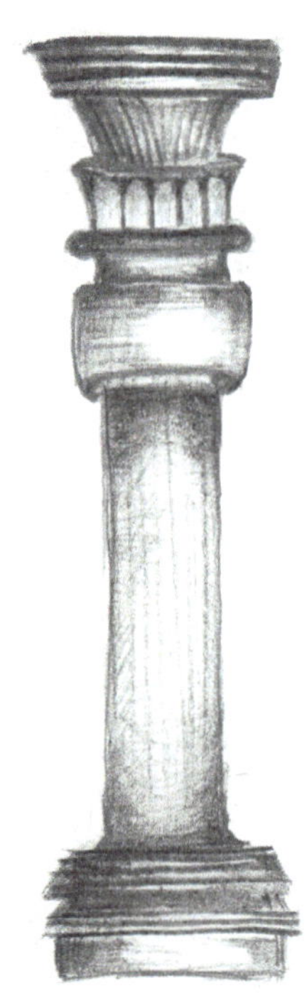

Correct term for sections

Section along the longer axis is called longitudinal section and section along the shorter axis is called transverse section.

Section for presentation should cut through the most important spaces, showing their heights and explaining relationship between different parts.

Section for construction documentation should cut through the most complicated assemblies and construction details.

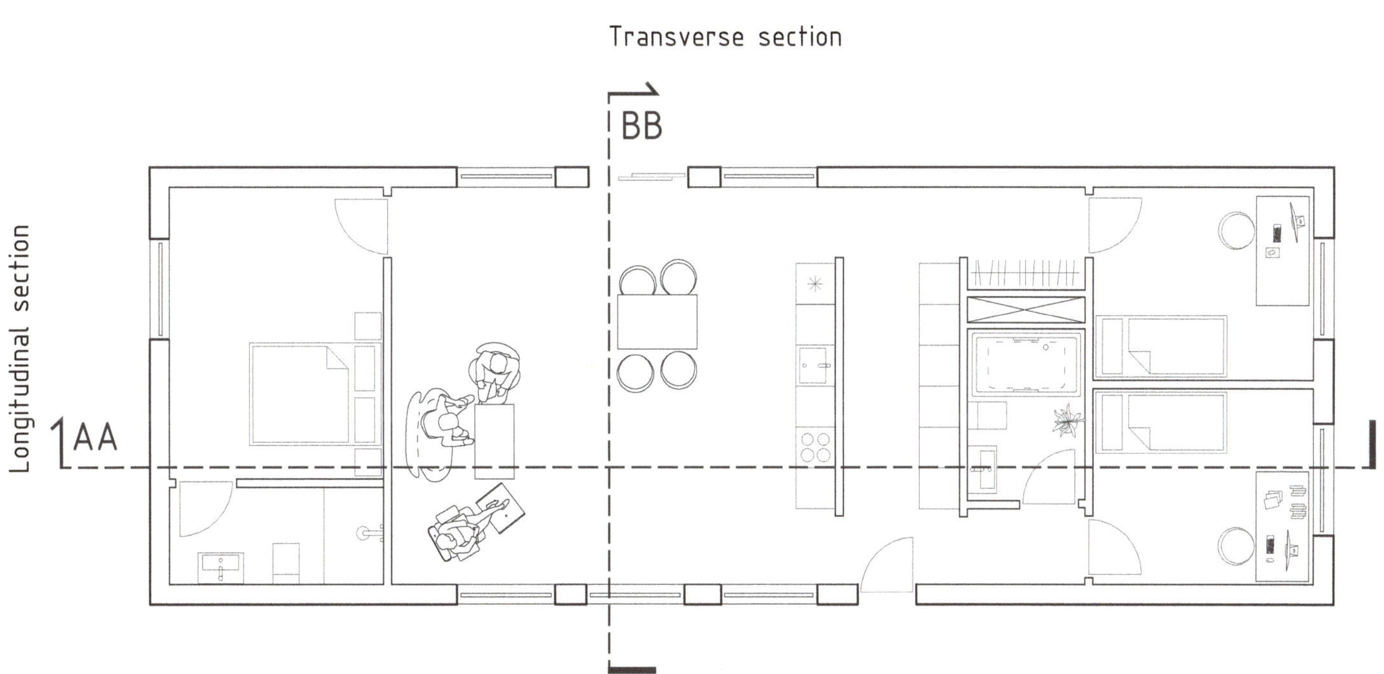

Do not forget the greenery

Trees, bushes, shrubs, hedges, flowers, herbs and other vegetation rejuvenates your drawings. The catch is to only use them if they are actually planned to be located in places where you draw them. Huge amount of architectural renderings nowadays suffer from excessive use of shrubbery, especially on high rises, even though the actual built environment is much less green than the renderings promised.

Show what you plan to plant. Lush vegetation is more than a folly to fill leftover spaces. Trees and plants clean air, reduce heat island effect, store carbon dioxide and promote biodiversity.

Make models

It is so much easier to imagine your design in three dimensions. Therefore it can be a great idea to make a model of your design. It can help you understand your project much better and show you new opportunities you can pursue. You can make a quick model digitally or use cardboard, polystyrene or whatever lies around. Show it to colleagues, discuss it and react upon new discoveries.

Design intention

Before starting right off with a plan or section, perhaps you can try to design a perspective. Or a room perspective. How should the living room look? How big are the windows, where is the sofa? This approach from microscale to macroscale can yield an interesting result.

Alina in Louisiana Museum of Modern Art | Denmark

See your own presentation

Are your drawings and headlines legible from the point where the audience will be? Is your presentation organized in a logical sequence so you do not have to shift attention from one part of the board to the other? You can also ask your friend to help you. Two pairs of eyes are better than one.

You can never please everyone

The more exact your audience is, the better. When you try to please everybody, you might end up with a bland design that appeals to no one.

If you curate the design for a specific person, it is nearly guaranteed the person really finds your work.

Rule of two

Every decision you make should be justified in two or more ways. The column both holds the roof and demarcates the space. The window allows light to pass into the room and frames the view outside at the same time. The stairs are meant for vertical circulation and can also serve as an orientation point. The more justification for each element, the better.

Design with intent

Every building has its own programme. Study it and adapt spaces to the programme, never adapt programme to a space. Different arrangements are needed for a museum, theatre, apartments or rocket launch centre. Start designing only after you really know what the requirements are, both explicit and implied.

What lies beyond the parti

In architecture, the parti is the primary concept or organizing idea behind a design. The most ambitious parti transcends the architecture itself. We do not want to create an architecture for architecture's sake. Parti derives from the story or philosophy behind the reason why the project came to life.

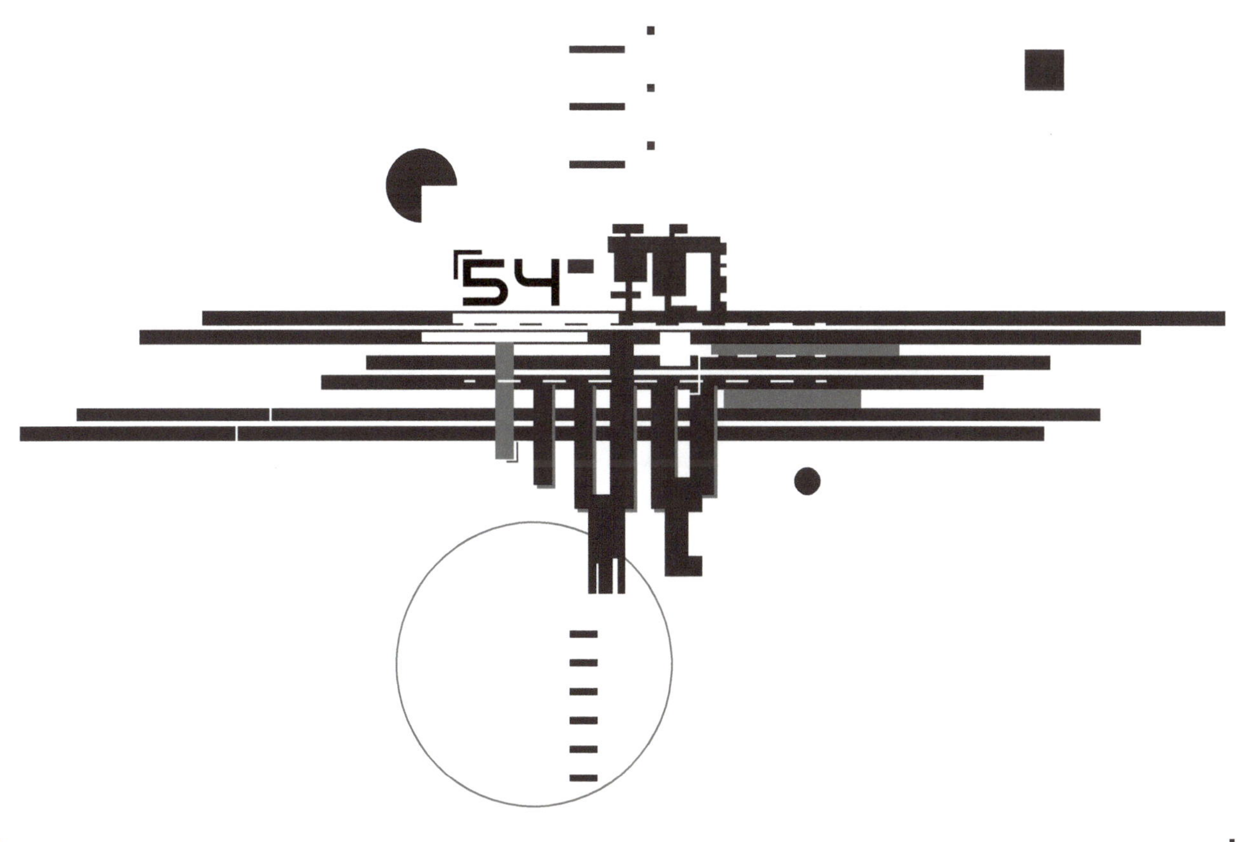

Fire safety

Multistory buildings must have at least two independent escape routes (i.e. two separate fire stairs). Ideally, they should be located at different ends of the building.

Learn how to compartmentalize the building to limit the spread of fire through the building.

Also, check your local requirements for widths of hallways and allowed materials for cladding.

Human life is more important than your design and fire code is different in every country. Make sure you know what you are doing.

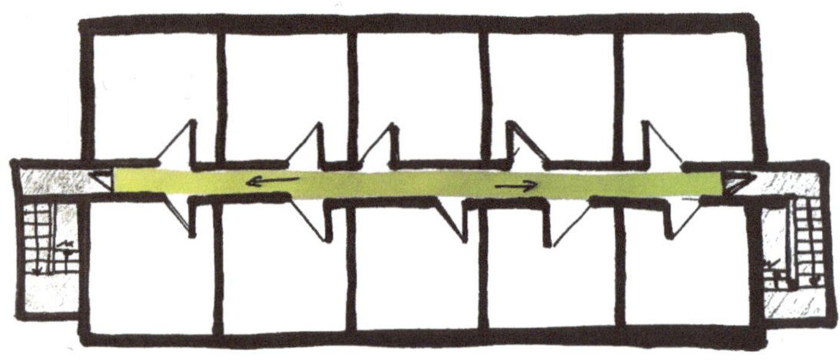

Counter the counterpoint

Counterpoints can be linked into a sequence of moves. One initial move can be countered in many different ways, that can be countered again. This creates a very dynamic composition with lots of dissonances. It can end up in madness though. Proceed with care.

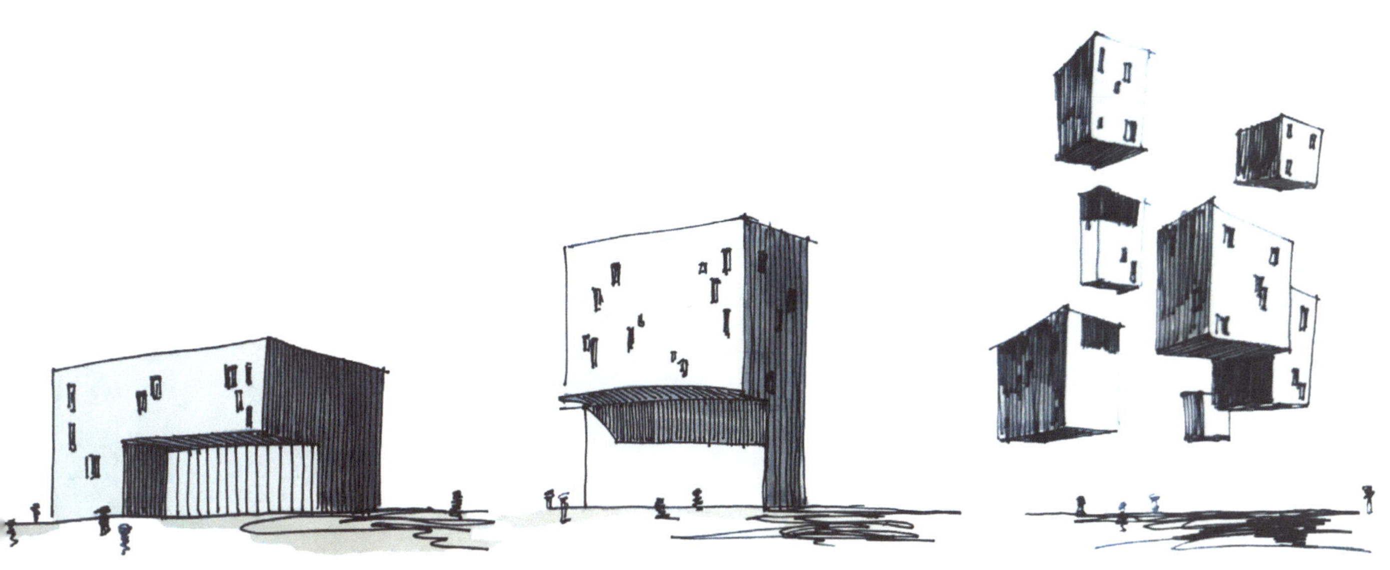

Via est scopus

Sometimes it is not important where you will end if you walk the right path. Make sure your every day makes you happy and success will come.

Composition in architecture

Static composition is usually symmetrical. It evokes firmness, tranquillity and permanence. However, it can also appear boring.

Dynamic composition is harder to achieve than static composition. It encourages movement and exploration. It is exciting and daring. Yet, it can also end up seeming chaotic and disorganized.

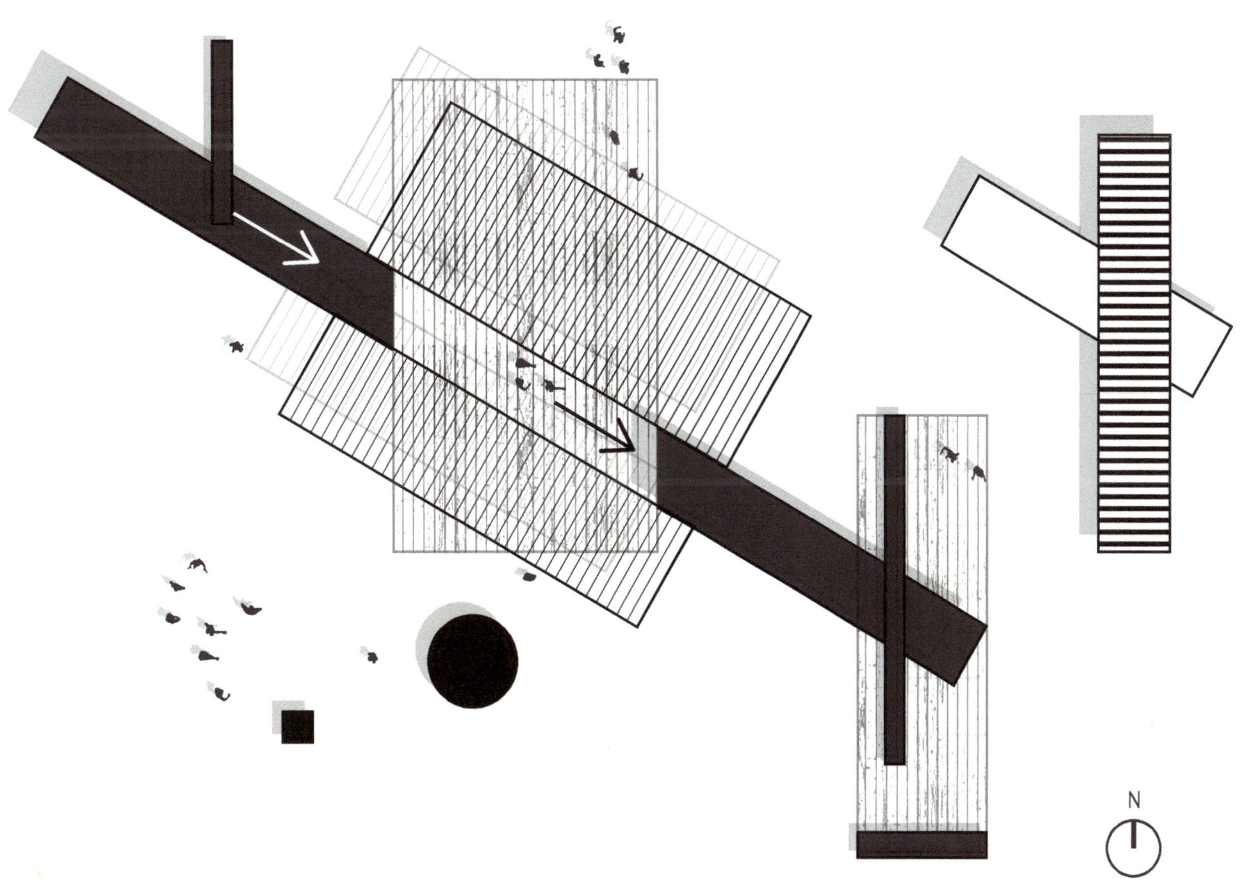

My way or the highway

Times of a lonely genius who can exercise the power are gone. Where Arne would have said, "My way, or the highway", how about to listen what people want to say and base the solution on collaboration. We are in the century of cooperation. Network and find like-minded individuals to create synergy. It is easier to get to the top together.

Organization of a square building

Square is a boring shape. Equilateral, non-dynamic. It can be hard for natural light to reach the centre. Therefore if you insist on square building, think about locating service rooms in the centre and circulation around it.

Or puncture the centre of the square. Doughnut is better than square. Create a courtyard flooded with light and protected from wind.

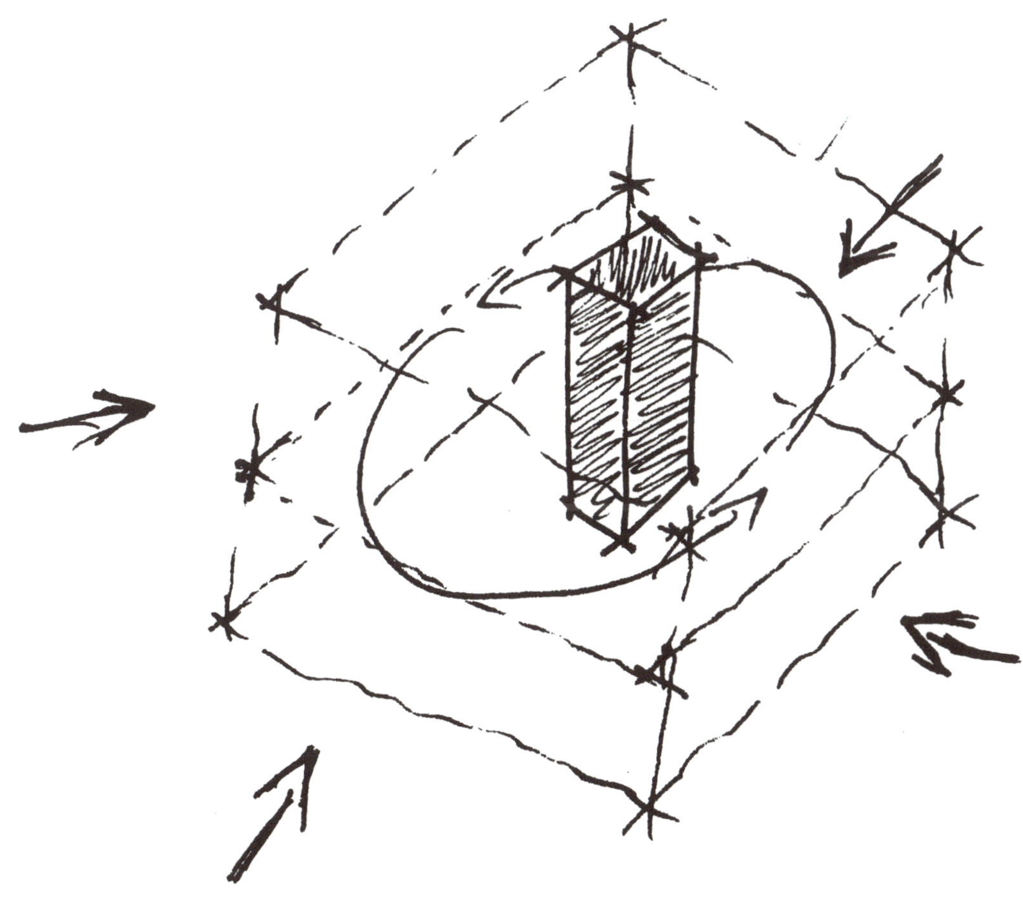

Story on A4

Our head is usually full of spectacular ideas, and sometimes we want to fit them all into our project. However, if you cannot explain the project on an A4 sheet of paper, then you are making it too complicated or wrong. The concept should be crystal clear and therefore easy to explain to anybody, even your grandmother. If it is not, go back to the initial point, figure out the core and trim the rest.

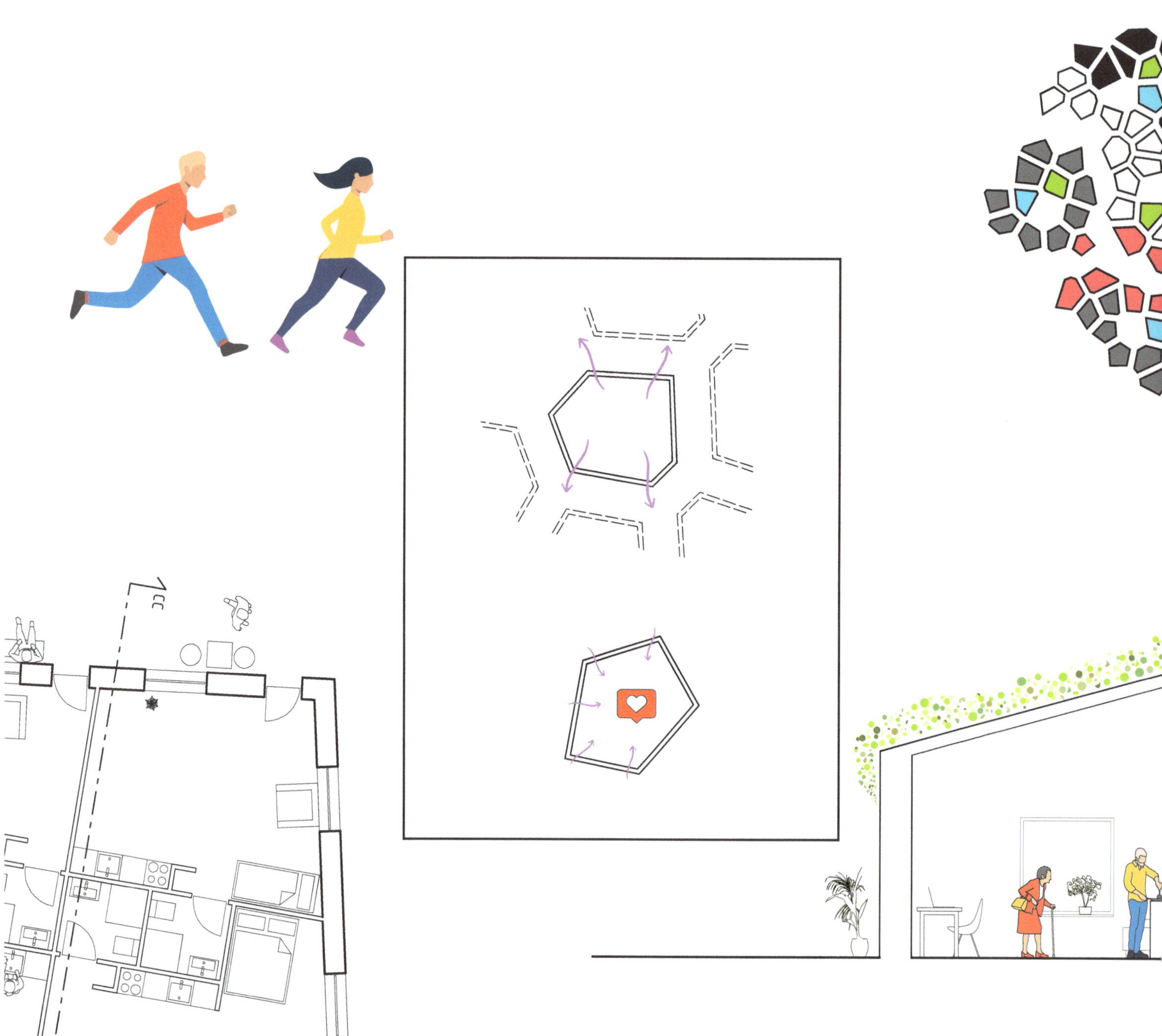

Polymath

Is a Greek term that describes a person whose expertise spans a significant number of different fields of human knowledge. That person can solve specific problems by reaching out to many different areas of intelligence. A great architect should try to reach this status. Anthropology, sociology, psychology, physics, urbanism, history, art, economic, politics, marketing, sales, entrepreneurship, statistic and many others. Architects can take information from all these sources and use it during the design process.

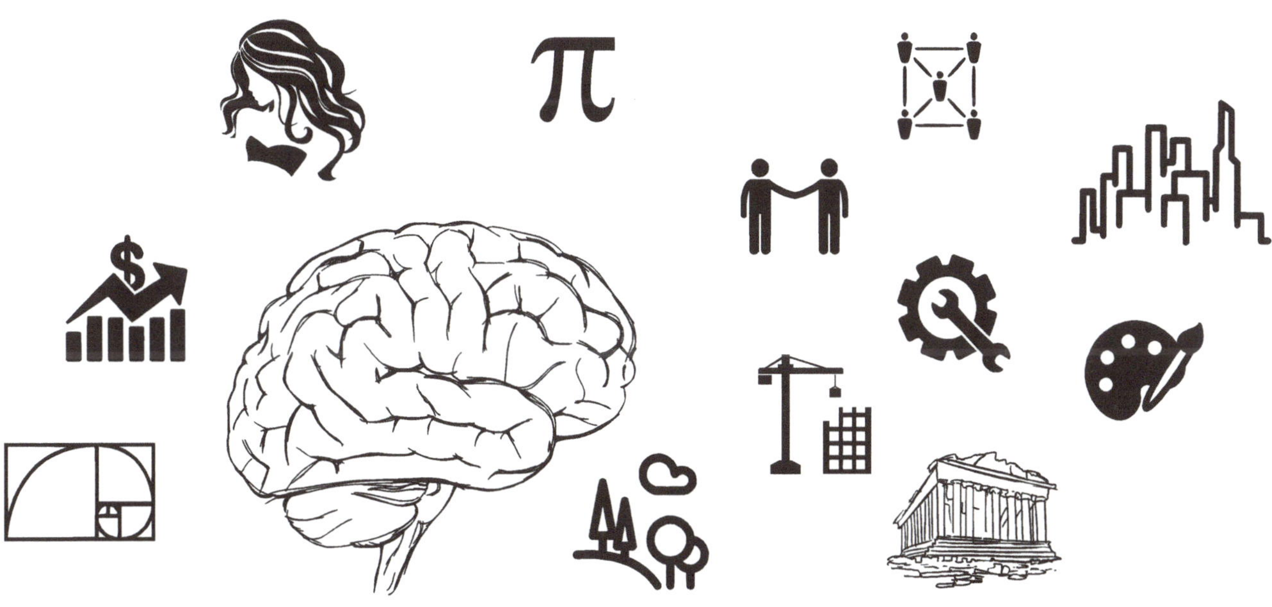

Ask the building what it wants to be

One architect asked his more successful colleague. "How come your design is so great and you get all the interesting commissions?". The reply was simple. "I just always give the clients what they want." The lesson here is to manage your own ego. Your ego is the enemy. You should not bend the building so it aligns with your personal desires. Instead, listen to your client and let the circumstances guide you.

Urban background

Most of the fabric of the city consists of background buildings such as offices or apartments. The small minority are foreground buildings. Those buildings stand out because they are important and that is reflected in architecture.

Secondary articulation

Spaces, objects and surfaces look better when there is a counterpoint to their primary geometry.

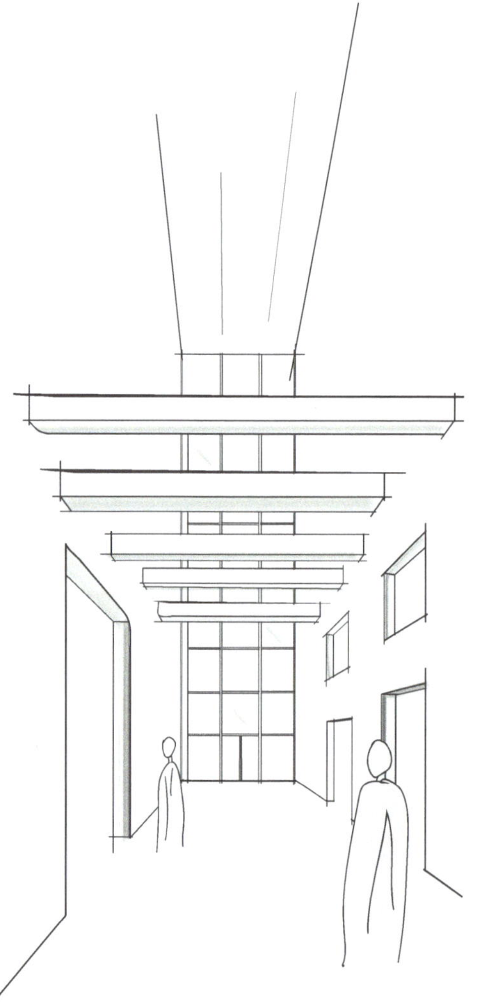

Harmonious composition

lies in the eye of beholder

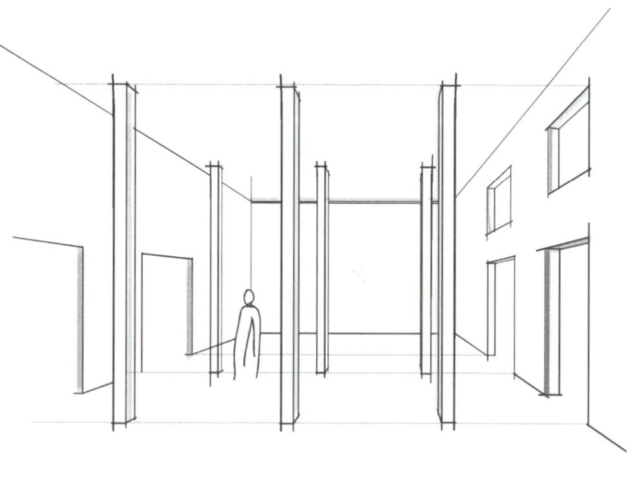

Use anchors to guide the people

Anchors are elements that draw the most people towards them. Reception in the hotel, department store in the mall or canteen in the school. By careful location of these anchors, you can guide people through other places, that should be visited more often. This tactic is used for example in shopping centres, where the supermarket is usually located at the far end, so you walk by other, smaller shops.

Way of design

There are so many ways to design. And probably none of them is wrong. What does that mean for you? It means that you have freedom of choice. You can find your own way. Design like no one else has ever designed or learn from your idols. Also, remember that there is no perfect way. Every process has its flaws, and that is fine, design should not be perfect.

Shapes and organization

Different shapes are meant to fit different programmes. Think about the activity that will take place inside.

Some shapes can be more suitable for your needs than others. Rectangle for an apartment, a crescent for a hotel, branched shape for a hospital with different wings. Try to arrange your spaces in few different ways and evaluate which one makes the most sense.

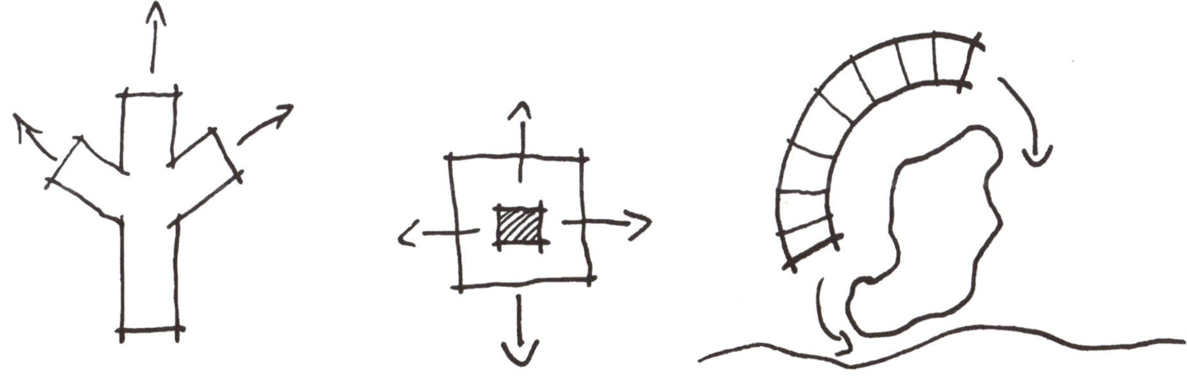

±10%

When designing, it is usually wise to inflate the area by 10% while simultaneously having back-up plan to scale it down 10%. Usually the projects go either of two ways.

- Additional spaces are requested from the client or technical rooms, unforeseen structural elements and more storage is needed.

- The project ends up over the budget and trimming down unnecessary square footage from hallways and secondary spaces is the best way to keep the project from crumbling down.

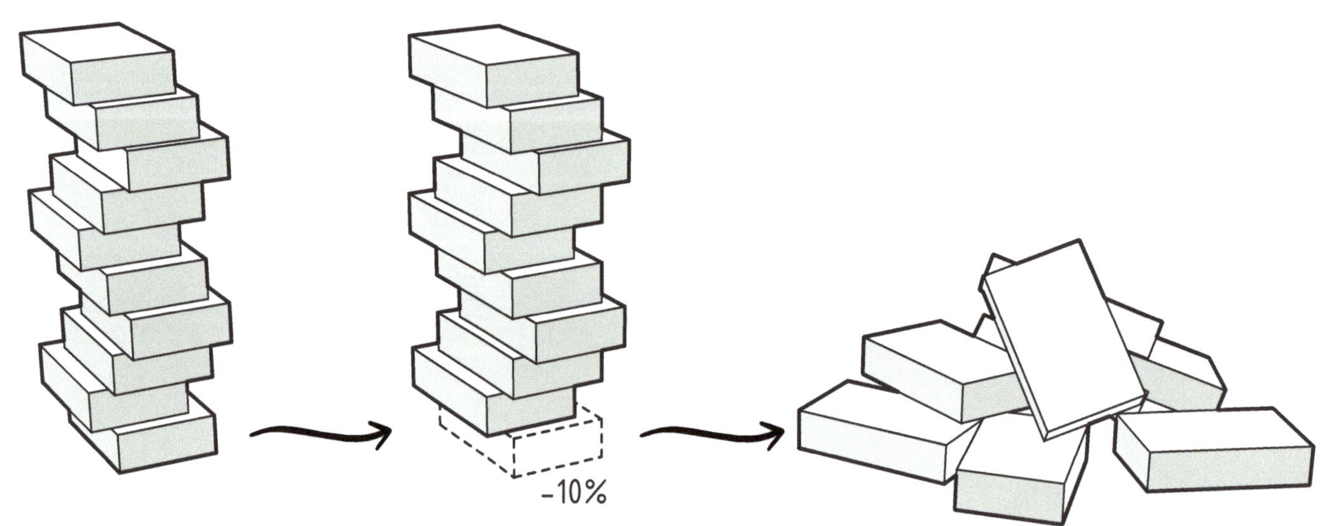

Underpromise – overdeliver

The world would be a totally different place if everybody pushed a tiny bit harder. A better place. Luckily, there is something you can do. Set an example for others to follow. As soon as you will give your best to everything you do, your life will improve drastically. People will appreciate when you lift some responsibility from their shoulders and many of them will reciprocate. Everybody loves to get something little extra, free or surprising.

The reward at the end of a journey

Our experience from architecture is influenced by how we reached the place. If everything is visible from the first moment, the interest quickly fades.

In order to create rich experience of arrival, try to offer a glimpse of place every now and then and take it away again in order to give it back a minute after. Slowly unveil the building and carefully curate the whole journey. Works best with religious, sacred or important places.

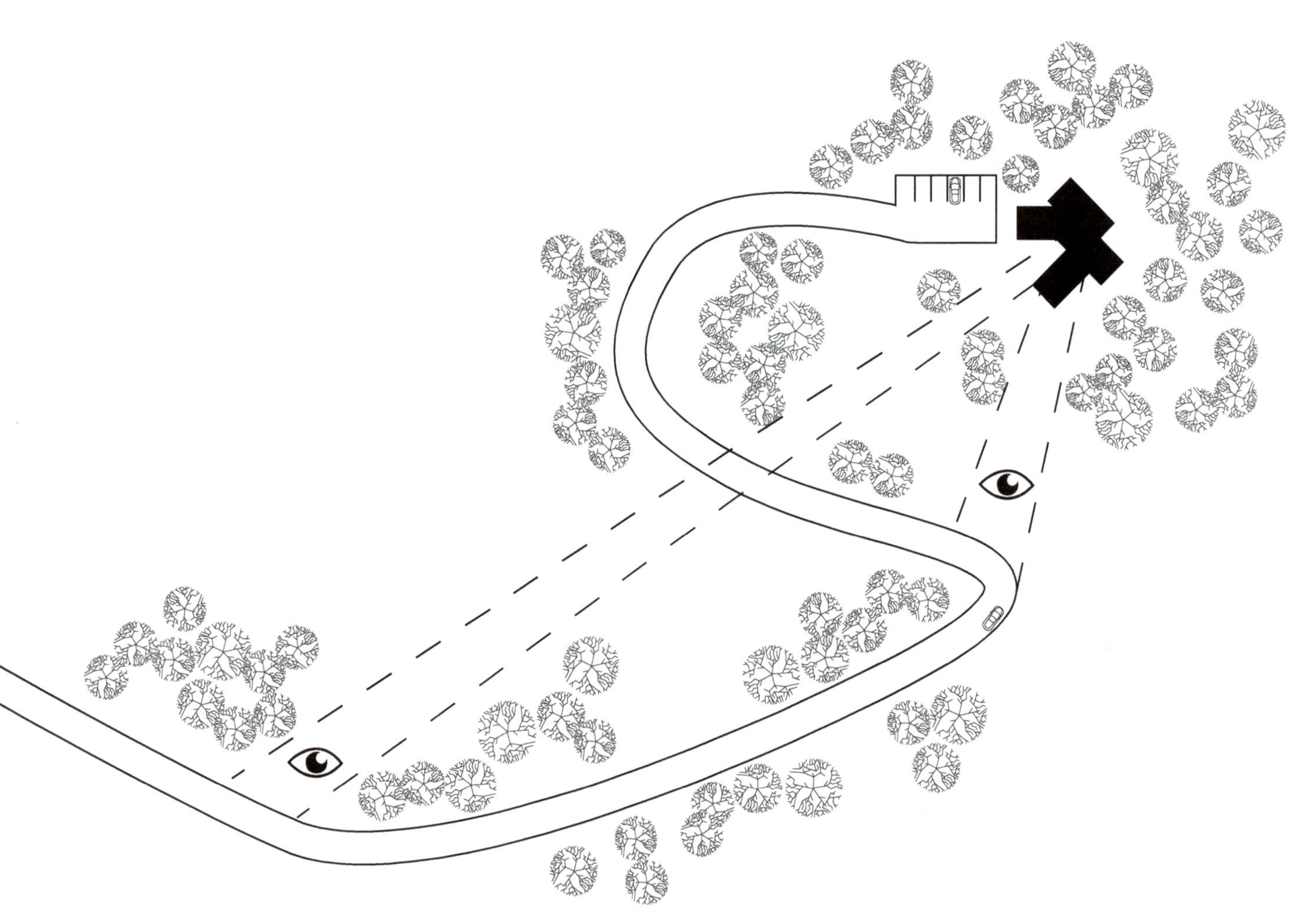

Know who the drawing is for

Your drawings are meant for many different people. Lots of them are not interested in architecture – at all. Engineers see your drawings as a set of walls, columns and beams, cost engineers see every item as its monetary value and clients might have a hard time understanding a drawing. Your job is to make every drawing understandable for the recipient.

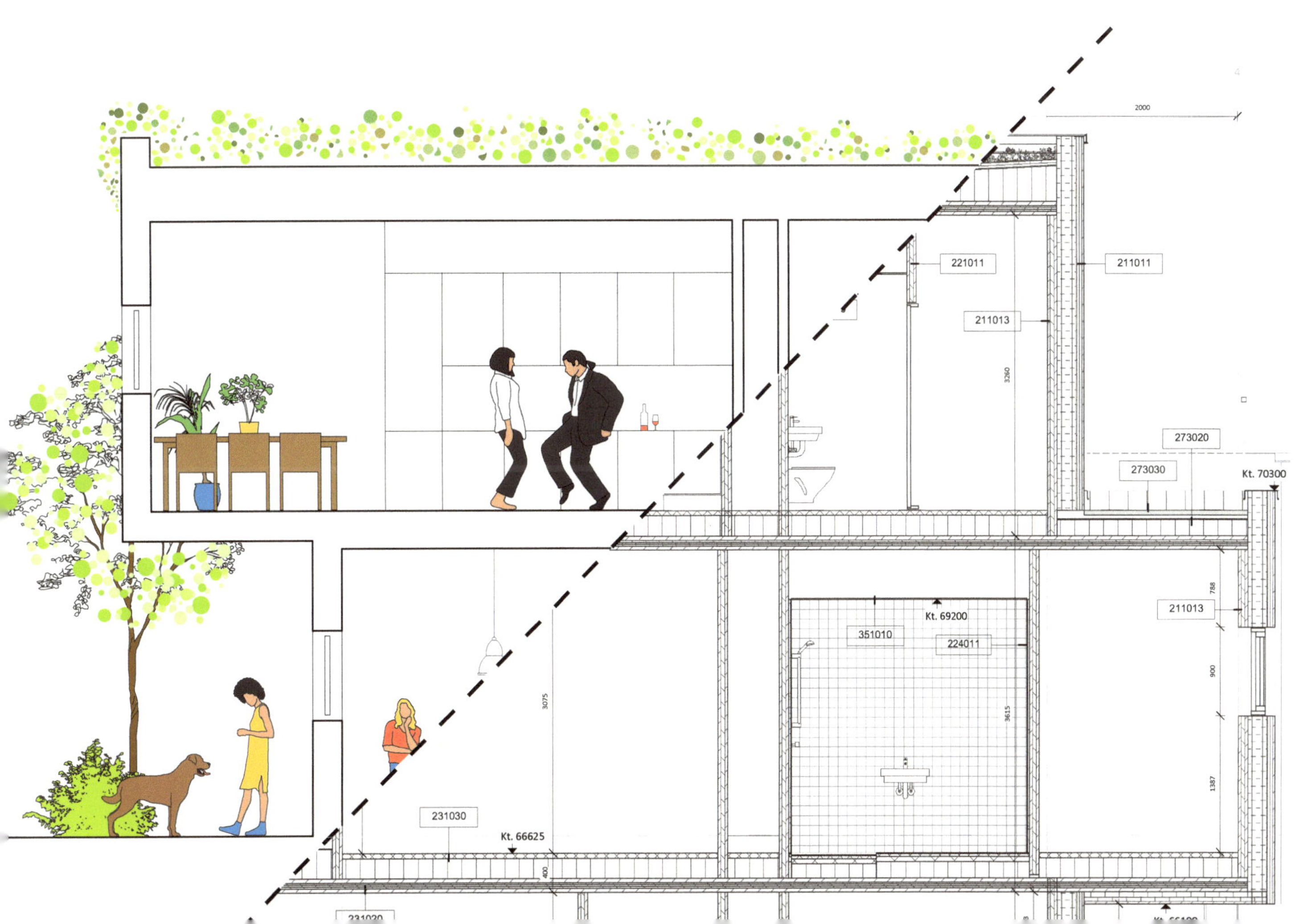

Create to live up to your expectations

You can doubt yourself and your capabilities, that is fine. Dissatisfaction with your own work is healthy to some extent. There is no simple way to overcome this when you rely on your creativity to support yourself and your family. What I do is to simply make things. Over and over, and with every step I am dissatisfied a little less. In that way, we can one day live up to our own expectations.

Final thoughts

Congratulations for making it that far. I sincerely hope you enjoyed reading this book as much as I enjoyed writing and illustrating it.

If there is one thing I would like you to take from this book, it would be this: Do not be afraid to try. You got it in you. You can achieve what you dream of and more. Even though, it takes time and effort, one day, you will see that it was all worth it.

Acknowledgement

Writing a book, and especially illustrating it turned out to be much harder than I initially thought. In fact, if I was alone, you would probably not be reading this book at all. Fortunately, I found out I am not alone.

This book would not be as boujee as it is without my dear friend Alina, who was not afraid to tell me it is not good enough and pushed me to try harder. You are the best. Thank you.

I would also like to sincerely thank people that helped me to create all those amazing illustrations. Alina and Alina, Barbara, Barbora and Barbora, Cristina and Kristína, Roberta, Sofia and Tsvetelina. You are amazing. Do not ever stop creating.

I am also grateful to my brother, Jakub, for his sharp comments.

And finally, I am forever indebted to my parents, Iva and Richard, who raised me to be a decent human being.

Additional resources and references

Publications
Andrew Watts, Modern Construction Handbook, 2018
Antony Radford, The Elements of Modern Architecture: Understanding Contemporary Buildings
François Blanciak, Siteless: 1001 Building Forms, 2008
Iain Jackson, The Architecture School Survival Guide, 2015
Lidwell William, Universal Principles of Design, 2010
Matthew Frederick, 101 Things I Learned in Architecture School, 2007
Zean Mair-Macfarlane, 100 Tips for Architecture Students, 2016

Online resources
Bob Borson's blog   lifeofanarchitect.com/
David Drazil's Skillshare class   skillshare.com/user/david_drazil
Doug Patt's Youtube channel   youtube.com/user/howtoarchitect
Eric Reinholdt's Youtube channel,   youtube.com/user/30by40
Matt Risinger's Youtube channel   youtube.com/user/MattRisinger

Podcasts
Life of an Architect   lifeofanarchitect.com/podcasts/
Midnight Charette   www.midnightcharette.com/

Image credits

List of lovely people and illustrations they submitted for this project.

Alina Croitoru   † 28, 36, 70, 93
Alina Komarnytska   † 65, 79, 83
Alina Lupasco   † 21, 48, 68
Barbora Chomová   † 94
Barbora Chotěborová   † 56
Barbara Maka   † 46, 75, 81
Cristina Bocaniciu   † 98
Jakub Slunečko   † 85
Kristína Pelachová   † 64, 73
Roberta Teisiūnaitė   † 34, 95
Sofia Marczuk   † 7, 45, 84
Tsvetelina Toncheva   † 14, 31, 38

Additional thanks to Bryan Maddock and his project Dimensions.com for wonderful architectural vector-based entourage, which was used to enhance many tips.

Thanks to David Drazil for guidance with publishing and his entourage used in tip 43.

I am grateful to architectural office TRANSFORM, for the permission to use drawings I created during my employment (see tips 4, 50 and 54).

About the author

Ondrej Slunecko is a young architect, artist and writer from the Czech Republic, currently based in Denmark.

Ondrej learned basics of architectural theory at Faculty of Arts and Architecture in Liberec, intricacies of construction at VIA University College, Horsens and complexities of urban development through courses CitiesX and Future Cities by Harvard and ETH Zurich.

His library consists of more than 100 books about architecture and he often participates in various competitions such as 120 Hours, Hypermega, Co-Life, Inspireli, Home or Habitat.

Recent practical experience includes working at offices UNION ARCH and TRANSFORM where he participated on various competitions including housing, kindergardens and cultural buildings.

I'm always looking for a great conversation, collaboration, or opportunity with awesome people. If you'd like to reach out, try these.

constructingarchitect.com

osl@bureauboujee.com

linkedin.com/in/ondrejslunecko/

instagram.com/bureauboujee/

facebook.com/lifeofaconstructingarchitect

Publisher:
Ondrej Slunecko
V Lucinach 651
463 12 Liberec

Published in May 2020

First edition
110 pages

ISBN: 978-80-270-7652-9
Keywords: Architecture, architect, design, urbanism, city, human scale, home, interior, construction